EMOTIONAL
EQUITY

EMOTIONAL EQUITY

7 PRINCIPLES
TO BUILDING A CULTURE OF TRUST
AND ACHIEVING SUCCESS IN BUSINESS

ELISA LEVY

Emotional Equity: 7 Principles to Building a Culture of Trust and Achieving Success in Business

For information about this title or to order other books and/or electronic media, contact the publisher:

Rankauf Publishing
Levy_elisa@hotmail.com

ISBNs:
978-1-7321650-2-1 print
978-1-7321650-1-4 eBook

Printed in the United States of America

Cover and Interior design: 1106 Design

To Stuart and Dale, who gave new meaning to the word "integrity" for me—and to their amazing families who follow in suit.

CONTENTS

FOREWORD

2018

THE FISH THAT DIDN'T GET AWAY

IN THE SPRING OF 1985, I was approached by a longtime law client of mine who suggested that I might be able to help a friend of his acquire a motel property in Key West, Florida. At the time, I was a managing partner of a mid-sized law firm in Southfield, Michigan, specializing in commercial transactions, acquisitions and divestitures. As it turned out, I had known his friend, Sigmund "Sig" Blum for many years. He was a well-known architect in the Detroit area, and we had memberships to the same country club.

Sig had been working with a real estate broker from Miami, named Sheldon Green, in his attempt to buy the forty-four-room Southeast Ocean Inn, located on United Street in the south end of the Old Town section of Key West. Sig and I met in my law office, and at the end of the meeting he asked if I would accompany him to the island to meet with Green and the seller. I agreed, and in July we went to Key West, where I was introduced to a run-down 1950s motel. To say that I was unimpressed is an understatement. The property was a block away from the ocean. Its two 22-room buildings were outdated and in disrepair, as was the swimming pool. There was a separate restaurant building on site, but it was vacant and badly deteriorated. Everything was surrounded by a barren asphalt parking lot. A picture of beauty the South East Ocean Inn was not. It also wasn't generating much cash flow, maybe $6,000 per room annually, and the seller was asking more than $2 million. Frankly, I couldn't imagine why anyone in their right mind would consider this purchase.

Sig, however, saw redevelopment potential in the property. He was convinced he could fix it up, build between thirty and forty additional rooms, and run a profitable hands-on operation. As a minor investor in a Holiday Inn in Traverse City, Michigan, which was generating reasonable cash flow, Sig had become enamored by the idea of transitioning from architecture to the hospitality business, and he felt the Key West motel was the right opportunity.

Sheldon Green, the real estate broker, recognized my lack of enthusiasm for the project and sensed that I would try to persuade Sig to reconsider. He was correct in his analysis. In an attempt to pique my interest, he mentioned that there were three other properties in the vicinity of the South East Ocean Inn that he had previously listed but recently taken off the market. There was the fifty-three-unit Southernmost Motel, located on South Street across from the ocean and directly behind the South East Ocean Inn, allowing the two properties to be easily combined. Across South Street, located on the waterfront, were the forty-seven-unit

South Beach Motel and the eleven-room La Mer guest house, which was the gem of all of these properties. Assuming Sig could redevelop the South East Ocean Inn as he envisioned, he would ultimately have a 127-unit property on the north side of South Street and fifty-eight units on the water, a total of 185 units. The opportunity suddenly looked a lot more interesting.

There were, however, two challenges to overcome. The first was funding. Sig did not have deep pockets, and with the four properties together, he was looking at a $9 million total acquisition price, plus $2.5 million in renovations and $500,000 in working capital—well beyond his original budget for the South East Ocean Inn. Financing was going to be a problem. So, I made Sig a proposal. My partner, Stuart Kaufman, and I would, subject to a review of the sellers' financials and the preparation of satisfactory financial projections, become fifty-fifty partners in the venture. Stuart and I had considerable real estate syndication experience and a great banking relationship. Sig would oversee redevelopment and operations, and we would be responsible for raising the necessary debt and equity to finance the project. To the extent it was necessary to give up equity in order to raise the capital, we would reduce our percentage ownership proportionately. We ran projections and the transaction appeared to be too good to be true—our projected returns were incredibly high. We secured $1.25 million of equity from Mort Harris and Bill Berman, who had invested with us previously, in return for 50 percent of the deal. The balance of the funding was a combination of bank debt and seller financing. Securing the bank loan was a challenge, because the AIDS epidemic in Key West was receiving significant publicity, causing our bankers to have reservations. Fortunately, we were able to allay their concerns, and we closed the deal in the fall.

The second challenge was our collective lack of experience in the hospitality industry. Aside from his small investment in the Holiday Inn, Sig had none, while Stuart and I had even less, if that was possible. The fact didn't escape notice. A month or so following the closing, an article appeared in the real estate section of the Sunday edition of the *Miami Herald* entitled, "One That Didn't Get Away." Sheldon Green, without permission, had given the paper the story of our acquisition of the properties. The deal had set a record for the highest price per room paid in the Keys for similar properties, at approximately $60,000 per room. The implication of the story was clear: Green and his clients had made a big catch, and we were the "fish" who didn't know better. As one might imagine, we were upset about the unwarranted publicity. Who knew what the future would bring?

This book is about our twenty-seven-year swim in the Key West hospitality business as the owners and managers of the Southernmost Hotel Collection. Our final stroke was reached in August 2013, when we sold our properties in another record-breaking deal—261 rooms at a price in excess of $700,000 per key, again the highest price ever paid per room in the Florida Keys. Elisa Levy, our cherished consultant, has captured the management principles, methods, and strategies that inspired our wonderful staff and loyal clientele who helped us achieve success. My hope is that those who read this book will embrace some of the values and principles we brought to bear at the Southernmost Hotel Collection.

—Dale Rands

2018

PART I

WHAT IS EMOTIONAL EQUITY?

THE END OF AN ERA

To EXPLAIN WHAT EMOTIONAL EQUITY IS and how it can transform your business, I need to begin by telling you about the end of an era.

On a warm August night in 2013, my husband and I joined the staff and management of the Southernmost Hotel Collection (SHC) as they gathered for a private event at the famous Hot Tin Roof restaurant in Key West, Florida. The evening was supposed to be a grand celebration to mark the historic sale of the SHC to new owners, and a chance to bid a fond farewell to Dale Rands and Stuart Kaufman, the two men who had led the hotel to heights of success that no one, including them, ever imagined possible.

We were also there to celebrate career milestones for Matt Babich, the SHC's General Manager, and Carrie Babich, Director of Marketing and Sales. Both were being honored for twenty-five years of service—and both were the longest-serving individuals in their positions in the history of the hospitality industry in the Florida Keys.

It should have been a joyous occasion. And yet the atmosphere in the restaurant overlooking the Gulf of Mexico was subdued. People filed in quietly, the women in colorful sundresses and the men wearing Cuban shirts. Despite cheerful servers passing cold champagne and lively music coming across the water from nearby Sunset Pier, a palpable sadness hung in the air.

That feeling only deepened as the night progressed. I lost count of the number of employees who made speeches honoring Dale and Stuart and wishing them well. Much to my surprise, tears flowed freely, including my own. In my career as a consultant I had attended numerous goodbye dinners for clients, but none had ever been this emotional. At one point, as several people around us sobbed, my husband leaned in and whispered, "What the heck is going on here? Is this a party, or a wake?"

Dale and Stuart seemed equally sad. Earlier that week, after more than a quarter century of ownership, they and their business partners had sold the SHC for a staggering $184.5 million, a price in excess of $700,000 per room which, at the time, was the highest price per room ever paid for a hotel property in the Florida Keys. But instead of celebrating like they had won the lottery, both men now seemed to wonder if selling had been a mistake. To them, as to those who had worked for them, this was no ordinary goodbye.

Dale summed up his feelings candidly, as always. "Stuart and I have owned many businesses together," he said, "and most have been what I would call a financial success—but none was more personally rewarding than this one."

Dale's simple sentiment captured the core of what made the SHC different than most business ventures: It was rooted in something that felt more meaningful than mere financial success—something important, something not often discussed in business books or MBA programs. Without saying it in so many words, he was acknowledging that, to him and Stuart, the emotional investments they had made in the SHC mattered as much as the financial ones. You see, as co-managing partners of the SHC, Dale and Stuart had focused as much on building real and meaningful relationships with their employees as they did on building a strong balance sheet.

As a business philosophy, the approach Dale and Stuart took seems to go against many aspects of conventional wisdom; and yet I can tell you from experience that the SHC's financial success, up to and including the record-breaking sale, wouldn't have been possible without the emotional investments the two men made in the business. There was a special quality about the SHC, a feeling rooted in the culture Dale and Stuart and their leadership team had cultivated over many years—a feeling, shared by staff and guests alike, that the Southernmost Hotel Collection was more than a hotel.

In fact, that feeling was the clincher in the deal with LaSalle Hotel Properties, the asset company that purchased the SHC. Before making a bid, LaSalle sent their asset manager David Danielli from Washington DC to Key West to scope out the prospect. The LaSalle team had already determined the price they were willing to pay based on the financial data they had received, and David's trip was intended to confirm their thinking. When David arrived at the SHC, he was immediately struck by the hotel's unique culture and personal service, and he recognized the extraordinary value of the special feeling they created. He went back to Washington DC and argued that LaSalle could and, if need be, should pay a higher price to acquire the hotel. In the end, LaSalle's winning bid was 50 percent higher per room than another Key West beachfront hotel that had sold just four months earlier.

"What David experienced transcended the cold, hard numbers," says Stuart. "In my mind, we got paid for our culture as well as our hotel."

Of course, David was a smart guy, and he wasn't making the call based on a feeling alone. The SHC was a profitable business with a strong balance sheet and a history of growth. When Dale and Stuart and their partners took ownership in 1986, annual room revenue was approximately $3 million; in 2013, they were projecting $26 million. Clearly, there was a profit to be made, if LaSalle could sustain the model of success that Dale and Stuart had established.

Though the Keys community was surprised by the selling price, the staff of the SHC were not. They understood the power and value of the hotel's unique culture as well as anyone, and their loyalty to the hotel spoke volumes: On an island where turnover rates are high and the labor force often seems to be coming and going through a revolving door, the SHC boasted unheard-of staff retention rates. Over a period of three years, only three managers of a twenty-five-member management team left the company. More remarkably, many of the frontline staff had stayed with the resort for more than two decades. The SHC was not a place people wanted to leave.

No one wanted to leave the party on that warm August night, either. We all stayed just a little longer than the restaurant would have liked, lingering to tell one last story or share one final hug, until people finally began to make their way home to get a few hours of rest before work the next morning.

After I said my last goodbye, I paused to thank the wait staff who had hosted us all evening. One of the servers was curious about what she had witnessed. "Was all this hoopla just because a hotel sold?" she asked.

The Ivy League-trained consultant in me would have wondered the same thing if I hadn't experienced the SHC's extraordinary culture firsthand. From an outsider's perspective, it must have been strange to see a room full of people become so emotional over a business transaction. But I knew it wasn't strange at all. The hoopla wasn't just because a hotel sold, it was because of that feeling I've already described: the feeling that at the SHC, people mattered. The feeling that everyone who worked there was part of something meaningful.

I don't remember exactly what I said to the server who asked about the hoopla, but I know I didn't stop to explain what I was experiencing. I probably should have, because talking about emotions and relationships is the only way to truly understand what Dale and Stuart accomplished at the SHC, and how it was accomplished. As they would tell you, the financial rewards can't be separated from the emotional rewards. In fact, it was precisely their attention to the human side of the ledger that made the extraordinary financial rewards possible.

WHAT IS EMOTIONAL EQUITY?

I am often asked by other businesses to reveal the "secret ingredient" to the SHC's success. They want a prescribed formula to follow that will help them replicate the hotel's customer satisfaction and retention, the top ratings on social media platforms like TripAdvisor, the high staff morale and low turnover—and, of course, the profitability.

I always start by telling people the SHC's success didn't come from a formula, but from a philosophy that Dale and Stuart developed and put into practice over time, a philosophy I call

"Emotional Equity." Emotional Equity is a people-centered approach to doing business based on a quality that is often missing from organizations today—human connection. It empowers leaders to build genuine relationships with their staff, and inspires staff to do the same with customers. Emotional Equity expands the definition of success beyond profitability to include a deep sense of purpose and personal connection to others. It helps everyone in a business find meaning in their work, from owners and leaders to employees on the front lines. The results are long-term growth and profitability driven by authentic loyalty from staff and customers alike.

As a philosophy, Emotional Equity provides principles and guidelines, not rigid prescriptions. This makes it flexible enough to accommodate an individual company's circumstances, while also being broadly relevant across industries. Since 2008, I have worked with clients to successfully apply the principles of Emotional Equity to organizations that range from hospitality to Fortune 500 companies, and even to international nonprofits.

This book introduces the seven principles of Emotional Equity and provides practical guidelines for implementation. It is intended for business owners and leaders who want to make their businesses more profitable and more personally rewarding for themselves, their staff, and their customers, as Dale and Stuart did. Emotional Equity is what made this kind of success possible at the Southernmost Hotel Collection. It can do the same for you.

EMOTIONAL EQUITY
AND THE STORY OF THE
SOUTHERNMOST HOTEL
COLLECTION

At first glance, Emotional Equity seems like a contradiction in terms. Many leaders who follow conventional business philosophies believe there must be a strict divide between their employees' personal and professional lives. Supporters of this philosophy believe that mixing the two can lead to inappropriate relationships and favoritism. Knowing too much about your people, they think, is a recipe for drama and unprofessionalism.

If that is the conventional wisdom, how can it be productive to talk about something as subjective as human emotions in terms of capital and investment, when the prevailing belief is that business is business and people should keep their personal lives and feelings outside of work?

The answer I learned from Dale and Stuart is simple: It's impossible to truly separate work and personal lives; any barrier between the two is artificial and arbitrary. Our personal lives don't magically go on hold when we show up for work, and our experiences at work can't be neatly compartmentalized from our personal lives when we head home.

Emotional Equity acknowledges this complicated reality and embraces it. Instead of expecting leaders and employees to become automatons at work, Emotional Equity encourages leaders to engage with their staff and build relationships for the sake of building relationships. This doesn't mean abandoning appropriate boundaries, ignoring issues, or tolerating inappropriate behavior or poor job performance, as you will see; but it does mean making a genuine commitment to an approach that values people—employees and customers alike—for who they are, not just what they can contribute to the bottom line.

Emotional Equity doesn't diminish the importance of maintaining a strong balance sheet, or appropriately managing risk. As Dale and Stuart are always quick to point out, Emotional Equity only works if it's built on a solid foundation; you need to have a fundamentally good business to emotionally invest in.

In the following chapters, I will introduce the seven principles of Emotional Equity and describe how you can use them to make your business more personally and financially rewarding. The seven principles are illustrated with examples of how Dale and Stuart and their leadership team at the SHC put them into practice. In order for these examples to make sense, it helps to know the story of the SHC.

1985–2000: BUILDING THE SOUTHERNMOST HOTEL COLLECTION

The story began in 1985, when Dale and Stuart, two lawyers from Michigan, partnered with Sigmund "Sig" Blum and two other investors to purchase four buildings in Key West, situated just off the island city's famous Duval Street. The properties included three motels and an eleven-room inn, totaling 155 guest rooms. Some of the rooms were on the beach, but most were not. One of the motels was in dire need of renovation. Individually, these properties had generated little interest on the Key West real estate market; but Dale and Stuart believed that the combined properties had the potential to be developed into a solid investment, despite a total asking price of $10 million.

Fittingly, the deal that created the SHC was as much a record-breaker as its eventual purchase by LaSalle twenty-seven years later in 1985; the $10 million purchase was the highest average price per room ever paid in the Keys for similar properties.

This caught peoples' attention. A month or so after the deal closed, an article about it appeared in the real estate section of the Sunday edition of the *Miami Herald* under the headline, "One That Didn't Get Away." Without permission, the seller's broker shared the story of the acquisition. The angle was that the broker and his clients had hooked some big fish from out of town and made a once-in-a-lifetime catch. Dale wasn't happy. "We were portrayed as yokels from Michigan, henceforth known as 'the Fish,'" he told me.

Unwanted publicity aside, the biggest challenge facing the SHC during its first few years was the fact that none of the partners had any hotel management experience. Sig, a well-known architect in the Detroit area, volunteered to be the SHC's managing partner. He relocated to Key West to oversee day-to-day operations and the redevelopment of the properties, but it became clear to Dale and Stuart that on-site management was necessary for the business to succeed.

In 1988, Dale wooed a young, dynamic couple, Matt and Carrie Babich, from Snowmass, Colorado, to Key West to assume leadership positions at the SHC. Matt was hired as the new General Manager, and Carrie was put in charge of Front Desk, Sales, and Marketing. Together they brought energy and enthusiasm to the management of the SHC, along with an understanding that customer service and staff team-building and morale were important to growing the business.

Sig didn't see the value of improving customer service or staff morale, and he was generally dismissive of Matt and Carrie's efforts in these areas. In contrast, he favored a short-term, strictly bottom-line approach to the business, with a focus on maintaining annual distributions to the partners at a targeted level. This was the primary driver behind all of his decisions as managing partner, from staffing levels and pay increases to operating budgets and capital expenditures. There were allowances for making improvements to the properties, including the initial redevelopment project that updated two of the motels and combined them into a single hotel with thirty additional rooms and a new lobby, pool, and bar; but spending was always constrained by Sig's goal of maximizing short-term profits.

While Sig's approach was good for the SHC's bottom line, it produced hidden costs that compounded over time. These costs came to light in late 1997 when Matt and Carrie informed Dale and Stuart that they were thinking about leaving their positions. The couple had been with the SHC for almost a decade at that point, and it was largely thanks to their perseverance and attention to detail that business was growing, and the hotel had developed a base of loyal, repeat customers. But despite this success, Matt and Carrie confided that they were losing faith in the SHC's future. The properties were understaffed, and Sig was reluctant to spend money on many needs, including routine maintenance. Guests were complaining daily, and staff morale was sinking. Sig's autocratic management style only made matters worse. When staff or guests complained, he often ignored them. Most decisions were made by him alone and were not open for discussion. Matt and Carrie felt uncomfortable going above Sig's head, but they were desperate.

Dale and Stuart understood that Matt and Carrie were integral to the business's success; losing them would be a major blow. Fortunately, Sig had already informed his partners that he was planning to retire at the end of the following year, and Dale and Stuart were preparing to take over as co-managing partners. They promised Matt and Carrie that Sig would soon be gone and things would change for the better under their leadership. They backed up their promise by offering the couple a new employment agreement that provided both incentives and equity in the company, in the hope that Matt and Carrie would make the SHC their career. The combination of the new contract and Sig's impending retirement sealed the deal, and Matt and Carrie decided to stay.

But the leadership transition didn't go as smoothly as planned.

In late 1998, Sig changed his mind about retiring and decided he wanted to continue as managing partner for another year. He didn't think Dale and Stuart were capable of overseeing the operation, and he proposed either selling the property or bringing in a professional management company upon his retirement. This led to a serious dispute among the SHC's general partners, with Sig unwilling to let Dale and Stuart take over management of the business. The fight wasn't primarily over money or even ego; it was a conflict of ideology over how people should be treated and how businesses should be run. Dale and Stuart had long questioned Sig's management style and his focus on generating short-term profit at the expense of long-term value—an approach that was pretty much the opposite of how Dale and Stuart had built and managed a number of other successful businesses together over several decades. (While Dale and Stuart didn't think of their own approach in philosophical terms at the time, they had been practicing many of the principles of Emotional Equity for years.) After much heated debate, the SHC's other investors backed Dale and Stuart, and the dispute was settled with a compromise that enabled Dale and Stuart to take over management of the SHC at the beginning of 2000, with Dale primarily responsible for overseeing day-to-day operations.

2000-2009: THE ERA OF EMOTIONAL EQUITY BEGINS

The leadership transition in 2000 was a pivotal moment in the history of the SHC. It marked the start of a new era that would see the business transformed from a cluster of profitable but unexceptional Key West motels into one of the top-rated and most successful resorts in South Florida, renowned for its customer service.

The SHC's transformation didn't happen by chance; it was the direct result of Dale and Stuart's commitment to the principles of Emotional Equity, which they began putting in place almost immediately with a series of sweeping changes to the organization's management culture.

Unlike Sig, their style of leadership was based on open communication and not only invited input from staff, but required it. "Empowerment, not autocracy" became the mantra. At Dale's direction, the management team, led by Matt and Carrie, began holding weekly meetings and daily department head meetings to ensure consistent communication throughout the organization, and to foster team-building and accountability. Dale and Stuart maintained regular contact with management to discuss goals and strategy. Decisions regarding most operational issues were transparent and open for discussion with stakeholders. When they were in Key West, Dale and Stuart walked the property, talking to staff and visiting with guests daily. They made it a priority that every department was adequately staffed, and they gave Matt and Carrie a mandate to upgrade the staff and to actively seek out top talent for key positions. Dale and Stuart understood what Sig's short-term approach had either overlooked or ignored—that improving staff morale and performance would lead to better customer service, all of which would be good for the business in the long term.

Dale and Stuart's investments in customer service and their staff were matched by an equal commitment to maintaining and improving the properties of the SHC itself. Right away they implemented a comprehensive program to address a backlog of deferred maintenance issues that had accumulated over the years, and between 2000 and 2007 they invested significantly in projects to refurbish the buildings, upgrade guest rooms, and improve the grounds. Whereas Sig's priority had been to boost profits by cutting costs and keeping expenses low, Dale and Stuart looked for opportunities to spend wisely to improve the customer experience, betting that increased guest satisfaction would lead to more revenue and profits over time. They were right. Guests noticed the difference, and so did the staff, who recognized that the owners cared about the condition of the property and the guest experience. This, in turn, created a sense of pride throughout the organization, and further boosted morale and the quality of service.

In 2007, the SHC reached another turning point in its evolution. By then, Dale and Stuart had succeeded in changing the organization's culture from top to bottom, business was thriving, and annual distributions to investors were exceeding even the most optimistic expectations. At this point the pair could have rested on their laurels, but instead they continued to pursue new opportunities to improve and expand their business, taking over a nearby restaurant and purchasing another hotel property. Together, these acquisitions would help to turn the SHC into a full-fledged resort and catapult the business to a new level of success.

The restaurant, located about fifty yards down the beach, had been a thorn in the side of the SHC for years. It was poorly managed, and the service and the food were subpar, ranking at the bottom of Zagat's in Key West. The problem for Dale and Stuart was that many guests assumed the restaurant was part of the SHC because of its location, and they complained about it bitterly to the Front Desk and in TripAdvisor reviews of the hotel. Taking over a 150-seat restaurant with a bad reputation was a risky move—at the time, no one involved with the SHC had restaurant experience, and some in the Key West community thought the business couldn't be salvaged—but Dale and Stuart believed they could improve the operation and use it as an amenity for their hotel guests. They renamed the struggling restaurant the Southernmost Beach Café and set about turning it around.

Dale and Stuart took their usual approach: They focused on changing the management culture, improving customer service, and investing wisely to increase quality. They hired more people, improved the quality of the food, created a new dinner menu, introduced happy hour specials and a diverse wine selection. And they made it clear to the staff that the most important thing was to offer a product everyone could be proud of.

With better management, better food, and better service, the Café rose to the top of social media sites and became a hot spot for hotel guests, locals, and tourists visiting the island. Over the next six years, net profits more than tripled.

The hotel acquisition was an even bigger undertaking. The property in question was the Atlantic Shores, a Key West landmark situated right next to the SHC. When the Atlantic Shores went up for sale, there were many prospective buyers. After much negotiation, Dale and Stuart struck a deal to purchase the property and make it part of the SHC. In 2007–2008, they demolished the old rooms and built an eighty-unit addition with waterfront rooms and top-of-the-line furnishings and amenities. When completed, the expansion would offer guests a new level of luxury that promised to completely reshape the SHC's identity.

And that's exactly what it did.

2009–2013: THE REWARDS OF EMOTIONAL EQUITY

The new and improved Southernmost on the Beach opened in February of 2009. With the project complete, the SHC now offered accommodations to suit almost any guest. There were upscale oceanfront rooms with private balconies, intimate guesthouse rooms, and more affordable rooms on the street side of the property. Guests staying in any room could use all the amenities of the resort.

Dale and Stuart knew that guest expectations would be higher than ever in this new environment, and they knew that their staff would have to be as outstanding as the resort's rooms, pools, and bars. They also knew that it was up to them, as the SHC's leaders, to do everything they could to make sure the staff were prepared to meet the challenge. To that end, they launched a program called Exceptional Customer Service (ECS) with the goal of raising the SHC's already great service to an entirely new level.

In the years that followed, the SHC's commitment to providing guests with great value and exceptional service earned it consistently high ratings on TripAdvisor and cultivated a growing base of loyal, repeat customers. Business grew dramatically, and profitability increased as Dale and Stuart continued to enhance the resort experience with new amenities and further improvements to the property. Occupancy rates climbed into the high 90 percents in-season and averaged between 88 percent and 91 percent year round. The SHC commanded room rates that were on a par with the most luxurious resorts on the island.

Through it all, Dale and Stuart continued to invest emotionally in the business. They each began spending more time in Key West, and they became more hands-on, working closely with management on every detail of the operation. They attended departmental meetings, and they were involved in every aspect of the ongoing capital improvement projects and all key personnel decisions. More remarkably, they got to know the majority of their 250 staff members and communicated with them constantly. It was leadership by example: The warmth, courtesy, and attention they expected their staff to show to guests, they showed to their staff in kind.

Which brings us to the end of the story—the record-breaking deal with LaSalle, the party at the Hot Tin Roof on that warm August night in 2013, the outpouring of emotions, the tearful goodbyes, the end of an era.

THE MORAL OF THE STORY

If you only focus on the financial outcome, the moral of the story seems simple: Be fiscally responsible and manage risk appropriately; create a good product and invest in it; train your staff and grow your business. And indeed these fundamental principles were crucial to the SHC's success.

But there was more to it.

Many businesses follow the same principles, and they don't achieve the same level of financial success that the SHC did after Dale and Stuart took over, either in terms of annual profitability or lifetime return on investment—even the SHC itself didn't produce comparable results during its first fourteen years, when it was managed as a strictly bottom-line-oriented business. In order to understand the exceptional profits and ROI, you have to take into account all of the things that Dale and Stuart's commitment to Emotional Equity created—the unique culture, the customer service, the loyalty of staff and guests alike.

Research in just about every industry under the sun shows that Stuart and Dale and their leadership team at the SHC had the formula right. Simply put, warmth and a feeling of personal connection build customer loyalty, increase staff retention rates, and have a huge impact on the bottom line. In a British Broadcasting Corporation (BBC) study conducted from 2014 to 2016, researchers found that customers' perception of warmth accounted for 41 percent of their willingness to recommend the broadcaster to others. A 2016 Gallup Poll found that companies with higher employee engagement were 22 percent more profitable than their competitors and enjoyed 21 percent more productivity.

The proof of Emotional Equity's effectiveness is borne in research and in the success of the SHC, yet so many business leaders don't know how to put the principles into practice, or even where to start. The difficulty arises from the fact that Emotional Equity emphasizes relationships and other intangibles: getting to know people, tapping in to the opinions of frontline staff and customers, shaping jobs around peoples' talents and interests, and showing care for staff and customers in unexpected and unsolicited ways. These things require a level of active engagement that many leaders have been taught to delegate or avoid altogether. To make Emotional Equity work, you have to come out from behind the computer, put down the reports, leave the cell phone in the office, and really connect with other human beings.

Emotional Equity can be replicated, but it can't be institutionalized or put on; it must be genuine. The owners of a Key West restaurant who heard about the success of the SHC hired me to work with their managers. I spent about four months coaching the co-owner, who had a reputation as a bully. I was asked by his business partner to coach him because the staff were fed up with daily verbal outbursts. Morale was low, and people were walking off the job. I worked with the co-owner on the principles of Emotional Equity several times a week, explaining how making a connection with his people, empowering them, and speaking with the utmost respect would make his business more profitable in the long run.

One afternoon I watched as he stood outside the restaurant, making small talk with one of his employees. He asked about her kids, he wanted her input on the menu, and they chatted about small things. He ended by thanking her for the good job she was doing.

"Great work," I told him, secretly patting myself on the back for having turned him around.

He smiled proudly and said, "I finally get what you have been teaching me—you just have to kiss your employees' asses and make them think you trust them, and they'll do whatever you want."

I stood there dumfounded, realizing I had failed to get through to him. The fundamental point of Emotional Equity—that genuine relationships lead to long-term success—had been completely lost. It didn't take the staff long to see through the charade. Turnover remained high, morale remained low, and the restaurant struggled to survive.

In contrast, I took on a client in the Keys that owns many restaurants and hotels. The owners had heard all about the SHC and wanted to replicate its success. They hired a Food and Beverage Manager to turn around one of their struggling restaurants, and they brought me in to introduce the principles of Emotional Equity. The new manager intuitively and genuinely embraced Emotional Equity, and he was more than open to any suggestion I gave him. As he began to build Emotional Equity with his staff and customers, the struggling restaurant rose in TripAdvisor's rankings from #30 to #11 in just six months, and went from losing money for two years to turning a profit for four quarters in a row.

I preach the virtues of Emotional Equity to all of my clients. And yet, despite being able to point to the story of the SHC and many other successes, getting business owners and leaders to follow through on the principles is the hardest part of my job. Everyone loves the financial results when they do follow through, but getting people in leadership roles to focus on relationships and authentically engage with their staff and customers is often a challenge. First, they subtly argue that it won't make a difference. Then they complain that they don't have the time, or that it's just not in their nature. These objections cost them staff, time, and ultimately money. They spin their wheels making systems effective, but not their people.

Emotional Equity indisputably leads to a better staff culture, improved customer service and satisfaction, and greater profit. And there's another dimension, one I didn't realize until after the SHC sold: Emotional Equity gives the leaders themselves a greater sense of purpose.

I saw this firsthand the day after the party at the Hot Tin Roof, when I stopped by the SHC. Dale and Stuart were there making the rounds with Matt and Carrie one last time. Dale was carrying a stack of envelopes with employees' names written on them. Inside each envelope was a check—a special "thank you" to each and every staff member. The sums were based on years of service and position. The money for several people was life changing.

Todd Jones, the SHC's Property Manager, came to me moments after Dale and Stuart presented him with his check. There were tears in his eyes. "You won't believe what just happened . . ." he began. The money he had received was enough to help him and his partner purchase a home in Key West—something they had dreamed of for years. Todd couldn't find the words to express his gratitude, and he wasn't alone—people all over the property were left speechless by Dale and Stuart's generosity.

When Dale and Stuart talk about the Southernmost Hotel Collection now, several years later, they often return to that day and reflect on how gratifying it was to share a portion of the hotel's financial success with their staff. As Stuart puts it, "It was a wonderful feeling to give to our staff in a way that I knew would make a difference in their lives."

It has been four years since the SHC was sold. Many of the employees have moved on to other hotels, but occasionally I run into them on the island. It amazes me to hear a front desk agent or housekeeper speak fondly and with sincere longing for the "old days" at the SHC. I'll see them in the grocery store, and in the middle of the produce aisle they will have tears in their eyes as they tell me the SHC was the best place they ever worked.

Creating that feeling of genuine connection for staff and customers is what Emotional Equity is all about. While there isn't a formula per se, there are seven principles that guide the process. As the story of the Southernmost Hotel Collection illustrates, and as you will see in your own business, if you choose to invest in Emotional Equity, these principles have proven time and again that they lead not only to more money, but to a greater impact on peoples' lives.

PART II

THE SEVEN PRINCIPLES
OF EMOTIONAL EQUITY

THE SEVEN PRINCIPLES OF EMOTIONAL EQUITY

EMOTIONAL EQUITY IS FOUNDED ON THE IDEA that people are the key to a business' success. Most leaders understand this on an intellectual level—they know that even the best product won't sell without a good team to behind it and customers to buy it—but when faced with the day-to-day challenges of running a business and maintaining a healthy bottom line, it is easy to forget that profits depend on how people feel, which in turn influences how they behave.

Emotional Equity is about making sure that people and relationships are central concerns of your business, not after-thoughts. This means prioritizing things like staff culture and customer experience—not at the expense of your bottom line, but as a means to ultimately achieve more profitability and greater long-term success.

There are seven principles of Emotional Equity:

1. *Get the "A Team" on Board:* Emotional Equity starts with a focus on getting a critical mass of staff that share a common vision for the organization. Hiring these "A Team" employees for key positions and keeping them requires creative approaches to recruitment and interviewing, and thinking outside the box when it comes to evaluating personality and potential and setting compensation.

2. *Empower Your Staff:* Giving people the power to do their jobs without feeling micromanaged allows them the opportunity to take ownership of their decisions and their work. We all seek independence and autonomy, and when leaders can give that to their people, it proves that they trust in their employees' judgment and capabilities.

3. *Accountability:* Managing a business well is impossible unless leaders hold their staff accountable for how they do their jobs and whether or not they meet expectations. Accountability is the feedback mechanism that reinforces individual responsibility and makes empowerment possible. It requires clear and consistent communication from leaders about what is expected, regular follow-up to ensure that staff are performing their duties, and consequences for staff doing or not doing what has been asked. When staff follow directives, they should be rewarded. Alternatively, if things aren't being done as asked, leaders need to immediately take corrective action.

4. *Actively Manage Conflicts:* When two or more people work together, some form of conflict is inevitable. How leaders handle these conflicts within an organization affects morale and teamwork, for better or worse. Leaders need to be prepared to get involved to constructively resolve

conflicts, to work with their mavericks, and to manage difficult employees.

5. ***Create a Culture of Care:*** Caring for others is the core of Emotional Equity. A business that takes into account all of life's priorities—health, relationships, and finances—will bring out the best in its employees. Emotional Equity inspires loyalty and deep-rooted commitment to leaders, co-workers, and customers, and it gives people a sense of meaning and purpose in their work. To create a genuine culture of care, leaders must foster healthy relationships inside and outside of work, support the physical health of their staff, and help their people grow financially.

6. ***Radical Hospitality:*** This principle goes hand in hand with creating a culture of care. It is about doing whatever you can to help your staff turn the organization's culture into exceptional service for customers. It's not enough to have standards and protocols; radical hospitality is personalized care and attention rooted in deeply held values, inspiration, and a sense of purpose. This is what sets Emotional Equity businesses apart from the rest. It is the key to being at the top of social media reviews and securing customers for life.

7. ***Provide Value for Money:*** Emotional Equity is a commitment to focusing on long-term value and investing in your business to provide the best possible value. Once you make the commitment, it changes everything, even your approach to strategic and financial decisions like budgeting and capital improvements.

The first five principles are focused on employees, and the last two apply mostly to customers; but what you will find is that all of the principles are based on the common themes of building relationships and putting people first.

The following chapters illustrate the seven principles of Emotional Equity through the SHC's example and provide readers with practical examples of how to implement them in almost any organization. The goal is not to lay out a prescriptive checklist, but rather to provide insights and advice that are flexible enough to apply to many different situations.

The seven principles build on each other and become a virtuous cycle: As you build your "A Team," they will become leaders in your organization. For them to take ownership, they must feel empowered and trusted to do their jobs. At the same time, there must be systems in place to hold people accountable and create a consistent culture. As conflicts arise, they must be addressed in a manner that leads to permanent resolutions, not band-aid fixes. None of these things can be achieved without a genuine culture of care and a commitment to creating a superior product. When employees feel valued as individuals, they strive to show the same level of care and attention to customers and to each other that leadership has shown to them, and thus radical hospitality is born. Together, these principles create a sense that work at every level of the organization is meaningful, that people's efforts matter and are part of something larger than themselves. This feeling transforms the business from top to bottom, improves morale, makes it easier to recruit and retain top talent, and increases customer satisfaction and loyalty—all of which lead to more profit, more growth, and more value.

The principles of Emotional Equity are guidelines, not rules. The goal is for you to take what is useful and apply it to the specific context of your organization.

In the end, Emotional Equity is the difference between making a good living and making a good life. It leads to financial gains that grow consistently over time, and it contributes to touching the lives of employees and customers in ways that we don't often see in business. That's ultimately what most of us are striving for—to make money *and* leave the world just a little bit better than it was before. The principles of Emotional Equity can help you do both, as they did for the SHC.

PRINCIPLE 1:
GET THE "A TEAM"
ON BOARD

Most clients I've worked with over the past two decades have treated recruitment as an afterthought. They know that hiring good people is important to the success of their organization, and they know that hiring the wrong people can have a serious negative impact in terms of morale and turnover costs, and yet they are content to go through the familiar motions of placing ads, reviewing resumes, and interviewing candidates. Instead of taking charge of the process, they push the paperwork over to HR and hope for the best. Why such apathy toward something so important?

Because, as many leaders have told me, hiring often feels like a crapshoot.

The first principle of Emotional Equity is about changing this attitude and getting leaders involved in the recruiting and hiring process. The goal is to build an "A Team," a core group of people at different levels of the organization who share a common vision about how people should be treated in business. Employees on the "A Team" are motivated and passionate about their work, and they care deeply about each other and their customers. These individuals are often high-performers in their respective roles, but job skills actually are not the most important factor to consider; the "A Team" has more to do with attitude and energy than anything else. Someone who is a good fit for the "A Team" can almost certainly acquire the necessary skills on the job and through training.

Of course, it's not realistic to expect 100 percent of your employees to be on the "A Team." What you need is a critical mass that will shape your organization's culture. The size of that critical mass varies from one company to the next, but in my experience if you can get 20 percent of your staff on the "A Team," your entire organization will be transformed.

In all my time as a consultant, I have seen few organizations that recruit and hire well, and even fewer that actively seek to hire an "A Team." Instead, I often see the afterthought approach, whether it's from a major corporation or a small nonprofit. The results are always the same: high turnover, a lack of creativity and energy from the staff, and, ultimately, low profitability. No wonder so many leaders think hiring is a crapshoot.

Dale and Stuart believed in the need for an "A Team." They, Matt, Carrie, and Adelheid Salas, the SHC's Operations Director, formed the hotel's Executive Committee. The committee knew they had to find their "A Team," rather than simply waiting for the right people to find them. Their approach entailed four key practices: active recruitment, innovative interviewing, favoring personality and potential over experience, and being flexible with individual compensation rates. Each of these practices helped Dale, Stuart, and the Executive Committee attract, retain, and develop the right people for their "A Team," who in turn influenced the balance of the staff. The result was improved morale and higher staff retention rates than any of their competitors, which was no small feat in a transient labor market like Key West.

ACTIVE RECRUITMENT

Here's how passive recruitment works: HR places an ad, and then waits for people to answer. Candidates who reply to the ad are screened, and a few are selected for interviews based upon the skills and experience described in their resumes. The candidates who pass the initial screening are interviewed, and the hiring manager selects the best person from the candidate pool that HR provided. The whole time, the manager has her fingers crossed that the process will bring in someone who has the right attitude, the right personality, the right experience, and the right skills, but she doesn't know what she is going to get until the candidates walk through her door. It's the equivalent of hanging out your fishing line and hoping that whatever happens to be nearby at the moment will bite.

Active recruitment flips the script: You identify the fish you want, and then you bring them aboard. Instead of waiting for candidates to come to you, or relying on a pool of applicants who happen to be looking for work when you happen to have an opening, you seek out the key people who will set the tone for the culture you want to create. These people may not be looking for a job when you find them; they may not be in your industry or live in the city your business is in; but there is something unique about them, and you think they are worth pursuing, so you make the attempt. Active recruitment requires leaders to be on the lookout for "A Team" talent all the time, to think outside of the box, and to be ready to recruit anywhere—while on vacation, on line at the grocery store, at the gym. It may even require creating a position that never existed.

Stuart and Dale used active recruitment to find and hire the SHC's "A Team." By the time they took the reins at the SHC, they couldn't wait for the right people to come to them. If they met someone who they thought would be an exceptional member of the "A Team," they would do what it took to get that person on board. They moved people across the country; they got them training to learn skills they had never practiced before; they found their spouses jobs in Key West. They also attracted the best and brightest in Key West. As they built their "A Team" and steadily transformed the SHC's culture, their reputation made staff from other reputable hotels want to come work for them at all levels of the organization.

The process started in 1988, long before Dale and Stuart took over the SHC, when Dale, while on vacation in Snowmass, Colorado, recruited Matt and Carrie Babich. At the time, Matt was the front desk manager at the condo-hotel where Dale owned a unit, and Carrie was working in marketing for the Aspen Ski Company. Matt was a hardworking young man from a blue-collar town in Michigan, while Carrie had grown up in Colorado, where her family was in the lodging business. The couple had married in 1985, and planned to stay out West and build a life together near Carrie's family. That is until Dale got a hold of them.

Dale visited Snowmass frequently in the late '80s, and, as is his nature, he got to know the people who worked there, including Matt and Carrie. He soon realized that there was something special about the young couple. He was impressed by Matt's courtesy, energy, and dedication to staff and tenants alike. Carrie was outgoing, enthusiastic, and engaging. She had an intuition for hospitality and was charming by nature. Dale thought they would be a good fit at the SHC, which at the time was in desperate need of competent people with hospitality experience to manage the day-to-day operations under Sig Blum.

It was an unconventional recruiting move. Dale had no indication that the couple were looking for new jobs, or that they wanted to leave Colorado. On top of that, Matt and Carrie were relatively inexperienced in terms of leadership. None of that stopped Dale from asking if they would be interested in a new opportunity in Key West. He saw that Matt and Carrie had potential, and he knew he could teach them how to be leaders. He told them about the SHC and encouraged them to interview for a job as co-managers. They agreed, more as an exploratory exercise than anything else, and in the interview they were as impressed by Dale as he was by them. They decided to give the SHC a shot. "I had no intention of leaving Snowmass until I met Dale," recalls Carrie. "But we were young, and he reminded us that life is about stepping outside your comfort zone." Matt became the SHC's new General Manager, and Carrie was hired as Director of Sales and Marketing.

In their leadership positions, Matt and Carrie followed Dale's example of active recruiting when they began hiring for the resort. If they met someone—anywhere—who they thought would be a good fit for the "A Team," they did whatever they could to bring that person on board. They stepped out of the traditional boundaries, took chances on people, and came up with creative ways of keeping people who were assets to the organization.

Over the years, active recruiting became the norm for the SHC's leaders. They recruited a Bar Manager, an Activities

Coordinator, and an IT manager from Detroit, a Reservationist from New Jersey, and countless other staff members from places they visited. These were all people they knew professionally whom they met on their travels or on vacation. It was risky to relocate people to a new place—particularly to the Keys, where the cost of living is high—but they were willing to take risks for the right people.

It didn't matter if the person they were courting had experience in the job. They figured they could train anyone if the candidate had the right attitude and the right personality to be part of the "A Team." As Stuart often said, "You can teach anyone with the right personality and intelligence how to do a job, but you can't teach anyone in a job how to have a good personality."

Sometimes, if they found a real gem, the leadership team would create a job to fit the person. "We didn't always have a position in mind," says Carrie. "But if I met someone who would fit with us, I made sure not to lose that opportunity."

At any given time the SHC had twenty to thirty staff who had been actively recruited for the "A Team." The leadership team still filled many positions in the traditional way by placing ads and collecting resumes, but at every level of the organization there were people who were carefully selected to be formal and informal leaders.

INNOVATIVE INTERVIEWING

The only thing a typical job interview tells you is how well the candidate interviews. Every manager has known the disappointment of hiring someone after a terrific interview, only to have the person bomb from day one.

The problem is that most job interviews are shallow and follow roughly the same outline from one organization to the next.

They consist of a set of superficial questions that focus mostly on the person's relevant experience to the job. The candidate knows what to expect and has all of his answers rehearsed. He googled "top 10 questions you'll be asked in a job interview" and knows how to turn the typical "tell me your biggest weakness" question into something positive, like "I tend to work too hard." This is fine if you're looking for platitudes, but not so great if your goal is to genuinely engage with the person sitting across the table from you.

Innovative interviewing goes beyond superficial, formulaic questions and past work experience. The goal is to get to know a candidate's personality and attitude, so you can judge whether that person is the right fit for your organization, and maybe even A-Team material. That means taking a different approach and throwing away the familiar script.

At the SHC, Dale and Stuart and the leadership team focused on authenticity. Their interview process went deeper, was more comprehensive, and aimed to capture the essence of the person being interviewed. I watched the Executive Committee members interview candidates many times, and even though I taught that skill in my own seminars and coaching practice, I learned a great deal from them.

During interviews, the SHC's leaders took the time to get a sense of the whole person they were interviewing, and they did it in a way that made the candidate want to open up. "I asked a lot of questions, but I did it casually," says Dale. "I inquired about education, background, their childhood, previous jobs, their hobbies, and I let the conversation take its own course. My goal was to understand their character, not just their skills. That was how I knew if they would really be a fit for us—it was about who they are as a person."

There wasn't a formula for interviews at the SHC, but there was definitely a style that the leadership team modeled off Dale's approach. The style can be broken down into three components: The first component was observing the person's personality, attitude, and energy. When making their final decision on who to hire, they often discussed whether a candidate brought enthusiasm and warmth into the room (a key factor for a job in the hospitality industry).

The second component was having a balance of behavioral and experiential questions. Roughly half of the questions were about how the candidate had handled or would handle certain situations with guests and co-workers.

The third component was spontaneous discourse. Most of the interview was a free-flowing conversation that was guided equally from the candidate.

When I observed these interviews, I noticed the candidates were surprised by some of the questions. If a candidate said they liked to boat in their free time, Dale would ask how they got interested in boating and what drew them to it, instead of nodding and moving on to a new question. It was this secondary level of deeper questioning that often led to more meaningful insights. "I always had in mind a list of certain questions I thought I would ask," says Dale. "However, they were in no particular order, and each answer the candidate gave me could lead to another, unscripted question. I let candidates talk as much as they wanted. The more they spoke, the more I could observe."

In fact, I remember my own first interview with Dale. I was armed and ready for the typical questions—and, truth be told, I wasn't looking forward to what I thought would be yet another go-round of the same old interview process. Two hours later I walked out of the room totally at ease and not worried about whether or not I got the job, but sincerely hoping I would keep in touch with Dale regardless. We'd had an open, engaging conversation that was more philosophical than practical, and I had genuinely enjoyed the experience—not something I ever expected to say about a job interview.

Matt, Carrie, and Adelheid adopted the same approach. "I always make sure I am two things in my interviews—casual and thorough," says Carrie. "I want the person sitting in front of me to feel calm and to be themselves. I understand what it's like to be in that chair. If they feel good, I can get a far better sense of who they really are as a person."

Like active recruitment, innovative interviewing requires more effort than the formulaic process it replaces. For the leaders of the SHC, the extra effort was rewarded with an "A Team" that helped to create a unique culture. The energy and commitment of the SHC's staff was palpable from the moment you first stepped foot on the property; guests raved about it, and the Key West community knew about it. The SHC enjoyed some of the longest tenure of managers and frontline staff on the island of Key West. This longevity contributed directly to the bottom line by reducing turnover, which can be one of the greatest expenses to an organization. It also gave the SHC top choice of the Key West labor pool. The organization's reputation was so strong that people new to the island and looking for work in hospitality often inquired at the SHC first, even when dozens of other organizations had positions open.

Innovative interviewing is worth the extra effort, if you remember that when you hire someone for your business, you are entering into a relationship—one that you hope will be mutually beneficial and endure for years. The leaders of the SHC understood that you can't start a meaningful relationship with a superficial conversation about past work experience. Their commitment to innovative interviewing helped them to truly engage with the people sitting across from them. More often than not, their innovation paid off.

FAVOR PERSONALITY OVER EXPERIENCE

When that pile of resumes crosses your desk, what's the first thing you do? Sift through and discard anyone without relevant experience. It's an easy way to quickly narrow your field of candidates. The problem is that you might have just thrown away the resume of the person who could have transformed your organization—an "A Team" candidate with a stellar personality and the smarts and dedication to match, but who doesn't yet have the particular combination of skills and experience you had in mind when writing the job description for your open position.

Resumes require reading between the lines. The subtext of a resume and of an interview carried a lot of weight at the SHC. The best example I can remember was the story of a pool attendant named Damali Phipps. After building the Southernmost Beach Resort on the ocean side, the SHC leaders added several new amenities to the resort, including pool attendants and an activities team. I was helping Matt with the search for candidates when we came across Damali's resume. It was surprisingly candid and told us right up front that Damali had been in trouble with the law when he was younger, and that he had no experience in hospitality. I was about to throw the resume in the "no" pile when Matt asked me to call Damali and set up an interview. I thought Matt was crazy. "Are you sure?" I asked.

Matt explained that for someone to be so honest in his resume, he was probably someone we would at least want to meet.

When Damali came in for his interview he was reticent, and it was hard to get him to do a lot of talking. Matt persisted. Eventually Damali opened up a little bit and spoke candidly about his past mistakes and his desire to start over; but by the time the interview was over, I had crossed him off my list and was already thinking about who we would interview next. I was dumbfounded when Matt turned to me and said, "I think we found our guy. We need honest people. This guy has been down the wrong path, and he is wanting to make things right. I know it's risky, but I think he could be a good fit."

It was another one of those wait-and-see moments for me at the SHC. I was sure I'd be proven right. Damali started the following week. Within days I was ready to eat my words. His attitude was great, he worked hard, the guests loved him, and he raised the bar for his peers—right from the start, he was part of the "A Team." Later, he would become the manager of the entire department. The guys on his team had a tremendous amount of respect for him.

Matt's hiring of Damali was just one of many examples of times when the SHC's leaders favored personality over experience and looked beyond superficial qualifications. Another came in 2007, after Dale and Stuart purchased the struggling restaurant adjacent to the hotel and turned it into the Southernmost Beach Café. When they took over the restaurant, they needed someone to manage it, having no restaurant experience themselves. Eventually they decided to promote the restaurant's assistant manager, Damian DeAngelis. Damian was experienced, bright, and energetic, but he had one major shortcoming: He had been trained by the previous owner, and had adopted the same ineffective approach to leadership that was at the root of the restaurant's problems. It seemed like a logical move to let him go and start a new chapter. And yet, Dale and Stuart saw potential in Damian. "We realized he had all the wrong habits from his previous boss," says Dale. "But we knew he had the right personality to manage. We told him that if he wanted the job, he'd have to unlearn everything he had been taught."

Damian accepted the challenge and did what Dale and Stuart asked: He became a leader who shared their vision of Emotional Equity. With Dale and Stuart's guidance and support, he went on to make the Southernmost Beach Café one of the most popular and profitable restaurants in the Keys. (After the SHC sold, Damian built a business of his own, purchasing three restaurants in Key West, and using some of the principles he learned from Stuart and Dale to turn them into a great success.)

Nowhere is the importance of considering personality in hiring decisions more apparent than in the hospitality industry. I learned from watching recruitment over eight years at the SHC that plenty of people can take a food order, make a good drink, or work a point of sales system; but not everyone has warmth, charm, a great attitude, and the ability to communicate well. Those are the people you want to look for and hire, even if they lack some of the skills the job requires. Remember what Stuart said: Skills can be trained; personality can't.

FLEXIBLE COMPENSATION

Setting compensation rates for your staff is a tricky equation. Most of my clients start with a vague estimate of the compensation offered by their competitors, and then use those estimates as the jumping-off point for what amounts to a set of arbitrary decisions based on a whole host of factors that often defy logic. In the end, the process usually boils down to a gut feeling about how much people "should" get paid. Mostly this means setting compensation rates as low as they think they can get away with.

Compensation was handled differently at the SHC. Dale and Stuart believed in paying people fairly, and they understood that in order to attract and retain the best people, they needed to be both competitive with their peers and flexible enough to pay more when someone was worth it—as Stuart often reminded me, "You get what you pay for."

The process was flexible, but rooted in sound research. Compensation rates were based on a comp-set analysis Matt did each month to stay on top of the market, which the leadership team used to set the general salary range for each position at the SHC. An individual's pay level within a range was determined by a combination of factors, the most important of which was job performance; length of service was also taken into consideration. In order to reward top performers above market rate, the SHC's leaders created supervisory roles within each job category, and people who demonstrated competence could quickly move up the pay scale as they became more experienced.

As with most things at the SHC under Dale and Stuart's leadership, pay ranges were never treated as absolutes. If the leaders believed that a person was an asset or had the potential to be, they would negotiate based on that, as opposed to a fixed, predetermined number. Such was the case for many employees on their "A Team." In particular I was impressed by how they hired their social media director, Lisa Malcolm. Carrie had known Lisa for some time, and she thought Lisa would be a great addition to her team. She actively recruited Lisa and brought her in for an interview. During the interview, Dale walked into Carrie's office by chance and joined the conversation. He knew right away that Lisa was the right fit for the job, and that she would be a great addition to the "A Team." The only challenge was salary: Lisa's requirements were higher than the position offered. When this obstacle came to light, Dale interjected. He remembers telling Lisa, "If you are as good as I think you are based upon your impressive interview, the salary won't be an issue." He didn't want her to get away, and he had created a system that was flexible enough to allow him and the leadership team to make decisions quickly when opportunities arose. It was a freedom most organizations don't allow.

"I knew Lisa could do something great for us," recalls Dale. "We always had to be flexible that way. If you're too rigid in salary or position, you lose great opportunities. I think that was one of the reasons we were so successful."

HOW TO BUILD AN "A TEAM" FOR YOUR ORGANIZATION

The central theme of recruiting and hiring at the SHC was flexibility. While there were guidelines in place, Dale and Stuart never let these guidelines dictate the outcome of the process. Instead, they empowered themselves and their leadership team to make exceptions on a case-by-case basis, to take smart risks, and to hire people whom other organizations might never have considered.

They also understood that not everyone in your organization has to be a superstar to create a culture of greatness; you just need to reach a critical mass with the right people. You do this by assembling an "A Team," a carefully chosen few at all levels of your company who will lead by example and set the tone for everyone else.

Recruiting an "A Team" is as much an art as a science. It takes effort, and there sometimes can be an element of luck involved, but that doesn't mean it's always a gamble. The practices Dale and Stuart and the Executive Committee put in place at the

SHC are a model for how you can shift the odds of finding the right people in your favor. A few small adjustments to your own recruiting process could make a big difference. Here are some things to try as you build your "A Team":

1. ***Active recruitment.*** Always be on the lookout for people who impress you. When you meet people who wow you, make a connection and give them your business card, get their number, and follow up with a phone call. They don't have to be in your industry; they just need to have the potential to be. People with great personality and great potential can transform an entire organization, and they are worth pursuing. Don't wait for them to come to you; go out and find them. Build the critical mass of 20 percent of people at all levels of your organization (front lines and management) who have the vision and energy you want your customers to experience. The more of these individuals you bring on board, the greater the positive impact on the culture of your organization.

2. ***Innovative interviewing.*** Re-examine the questions you and other leaders in your organization ask during interviews. Practice interviewing through casual conversation. Ask candidates about their dreams, hopes, and aspirations, and their past experiences outside of work. Imagine you had been given thirty minutes to really get a sense of who they are, and let their technical expertise be the last thing you ask about. Give them real-life situations that come up in the job and ask how they would handle them. Your goal should be to get to know job candidates as people, not only as professionals. Make your interviews more casual and try to put the candidates at ease; the more relaxed people are, the more their true personality will emerge. Whenever

possible, have a candidate interview with multiple people in your organization. Weighing the different perspectives will help you to form a more complete picture of the candidate.

3. *Personality and potential.* Whether you are reviewing resumes or interviewing candidates, narrow your focus to personality and potential rather than skills and experience. Of course, certain baseline skills are required for specific positions, but Dale and Stuart found time and again that a person's skills and experience are less important than attitude and personality. You can teach someone the skills necessary to do a job; you can't change personality. Make your interviews more casual and try to put the candidates at ease; the more relaxed people are, the more their true personality will emerge.

4. *Pay people, not positions.* Don't let your pay structure cause you to rule out great candidates or lose top performers. Establish guidelines and set appropriate ranges that reflect fair-market rates, but allow for flexibility on a case-by-case basis. Be willing to step outside your pay structure to get the right people on your "A Team," and to keep them.

PRINCIPLE 2:
EMPOWERMENT

GETTING THE RIGHT PEOPLE ON THE BUS doesn't mean you will keep them there. Many companies address employee retention with stock options, prime parking spots, bonuses, and elaborate reward strategies based on years of service, but they still don't retain staff effectively.

Employee retention is critical to profitability. First, the costs of hiring and training new staff have a significant impact on the bottom line. Second, without continuity, there is a lack of institutional knowledge. High turnover almost invariably leads to confusion and chaos. Customers are the first to feel it, and they choose to go elsewhere.

One of the simplest and most effective ways to retain employees is to empower them. Empowerment works because it meets a fundamental human need for autonomy and independence, and because we all feel more engaged when we have the power to make decisions. Thinking of staff as stakeholders instead of just frontline employees is a game-changer. The concept isn't new. In the 1970s and '80s many organizations adopted the idea of "inverted pyramids" and "horizontal structures" of leadership. Both approaches dismantled traditional, top-down business management hierarchies in which the head boss called all the shots and everyone else did as they were told. The shift came from the understanding that when employees have more of a say, they care more, work harder and do a better job—it is human nature to be invested in what we feel we have ownership over. Buzzwords like "empowerment" and "stakeholders" became part of the corporate language.

Semco, a global manufacturer based in Brazil, was a pioneer of these efforts. When Ricardo Semler, the twenty-something son of a factory owner, took over his father's struggling business, he did away with the organization's tight rules, empowered the company's workers to make decisions, and abolished all unnecessary red tape. He even allowed his front lines to decorate the buildings in which they worked. After all, he concluded, if they were going to spend their time there, they should have more input.

The result was a culture in which employees at all levels felt confident making decisions. Morale and productivity increased, and people worked harder than ever before. Within less than a decade Semco's profits soared beyond Semler's own ambitious goals, growing sixfold.

Many businesses have tried to follow the empowerment path by becoming more horizontal, but the transformation isn't as easy in practice as it seems in principle. Like most theories, the idea sounds great, but something gets lost in translation. In my own work, I have met dozens of corporate leaders who have handed me a business card with only their name printed on it, and no title. They explain with pride that their company has a flat organizational structure, yet as we talk it becomes clear that their leadership style remains top-down. They make unnecessary policies that bind their staff; they rarely ask for input; they rule with an iron fist. On the rare occasion that they show up on the front lines, employees assume it's to fire someone. In these organizations, horizontal is the new vertical.

About two years ago, I began working with a medium-sized hotel chain in South Florida. They were mediocre at best. Staff turnover was high and revenue was relatively low, despite operating in a robust market. The CEO sat across from me in his casual polo shirt and described a horizontal management structure in so many words. He had no title on his business card, and the managers who ran the departments spoke the same language of empowerment as the CEO. From the executive suite, the picture of the company was ideal.

The view from the front lines was entirely different. Morale was low. Despite all the talk of empowerment, the staff had very little decision-making authority. The managers had made more rules than anyone could remember having in the past, and they exercised tight control over every aspect of the business, so as to "keep everyone honest," as one manager told me. It was exactly the opposite of the culture they claimed to have embraced.

In my experience, businesses that try to institutionalize by being "non-institutional" yield worse results than organizations with an openly hierarchical approach. When what is preached is not practiced, people feel duped, which quickly leads to frustrated and demoralized employees.

The SHC was the opposite in every way. Dale and Stuart didn't use buzzwords like "horizontal structure," and they didn't spend time obsessing over management theories or formal systems. Instead, they did what seemed logical to them.

This isn't to say that the SHC operated without policies and procedures. On the contrary, the leaders made clear what their directives were (see: Principle 3: Accountability), and they expected their staff to follow those directives. But individual staff members were given wide latitude when it came to how they fulfilled their job responsibilities and responded to guest needs. Employees weren't burdened with red tape or limited by strict rules. In fact, if a rule wasn't absolutely necessary, it didn't exist. The SHC's leaders trusted their people to make good decisions on a daily basis, and they told them as much.

"The Executive Committee gave us the freedom to please the guests as they saw fit," explains former HR Manager and Controller Teresa Ross. This freedom made people genuinely care about their jobs and connect with the guests. "It wasn't uncommon to see our staff step out from behind the front desk or the bar to give our guests a hug. Our staff genuinely wanted to connect because they realized they had a lot of power. They could be themselves."

Unless they thought a staff member had made an egregious error, the Executive Committee supported almost every decision their frontline staff made. When people came to Stuart to ask about a guest issue, he often reminded people to use their own best judgment. "Chances are," he would say jokingly, "you won't make a decision that will put us out of business."

"They backed our decisions," explains former Front Desk Manager Elizabeth Patrick. "They wanted everyone to feel that we had authority. Our hands were never tied."

Working with the SHC, I learned that real empowerment is based on four things: letting people make decisions themselves;

eliminating unnecessary systems and rules; trusting in your people's integrity; and inviting debate. These practices, like most of what they did at the SHC, came naturally to Dale and Stuart. The result was a leadership approach that genuinely empowered their staff.

LET PEOPLE FIX PROBLEMS

Imagine you are working the front desk of a hotel and a travel-weary, angry customer is standing in front of you, refusing to stay in his room. This, he complains, is his one and only annual vacation, and he has traveled with his family for an entire day. He was "promised" a room with a king bed and a beach view, and he got neither. He demands a change immediately. You know from looking up the details that the mistake was his, but trying to convince him of that won't change the fact that he didn't get the vacation he had hoped for.

You happen to have a gorgeous oceanfront suite available. You can turn the situation around completely by giving him a free upgrade. The only problem is that if you do it, you'll get a call minutes later from the Revenue Manager, asking you to justify your decision, and reprimanding you for your actions. You will also have to fill out a three-page report to make your case. It will all be on camera, of course, to make sure there was no foul play.

You weigh your options: You can either deal with the angry guy for a few minutes, or subject yourself to all the other headaches you would have to endure to fix the problem. You choose the lesser of the two evils, and tell the guy in so many words that he's out of luck.

This scenario is common in bureaucratic environments. Employees can't do what they know is right without suffering the consequences. Their hands are tied, and it slowly erodes morale. Social media scores decline and eventually profit does too. The rules that prevent staff from making independent decisions place them directly at odds with the customer in difficult situations. Then they are criticized by management for not giving better service.

In contrast, the SHC built its reputation by being on the side its customers. Dale and Stuart made it 100 percent clear that when it came to serving customers, the front lines had the power to fix problems. There were times when it was appropriate to give away the oceanfront suite, and times when it was not; the decision was left up to the people who were dealing with the situation. Frontline staff were encouraged to talk to a manager if they were in doubt, but no one was required to get approval in advance, or to fill out paperwork to justify their decisions after the fact.

This empowerment applied to all facets of guest service at the SHC, not just to addressing complaints and resolving problems. If the staff thought of something that would make a guest's stay better, they had the authority to do it. This translated into many simple yet thoughtful acts of kindness. Guest Edye Baker recalled one such action taken by Darlene Ashcroft, an innkeeper at Dewy House. "We had come to the SHC a few times and always brought a jigsaw puzzle. My husband and I liked to sit on the porch in the afternoon by the beach and do a puzzle to relax. I'm not sure how Darlene even remembered this, but on our second trip, and every trip thereafter, there were new puzzles waiting for us." This thoughtful touch made a big impression on Ms. Baker and her husband. "We are VIP Diamond Members with Hilton, so we stay for free every time we travel. But we like the SHC for things like this so much that we forgo the free room and stay there."

Two of the world's most famous hotel chains, the Oberoi and the Ritz Carlton, take a similar approach. At the Oberoi, management requires front lines to do whatever it takes to delight guests. Some years ago, I was in the Oberoi's restaurant in Agra, India, and mentioned to the server I couldn't decide between two entrees. He insisted on having the kitchen make me a sample of both at no charge so that I could have the "perfect meal." I later asked the restaurant manager if they do that as a protocol when guests can't decide. He laughed and told me that the directive is far simpler than that: "Just delight every person you see."

The Ritz Carlton offers each staff member a sizable allowance to use at will to ensure a fantastic guest experience. Staff can spend their allowance money on items for guests, send something to their rooms, or offer a complimentary amenity or service.

The SHC had far fewer resources than these two major hotel chains, but that didn't stop them from empowering their staff to delight their guests. There was no specific formula or amount of money for staff to spend. The goal was to act from the heart, whatever that meant in a given situation. No two guests or situations were alike, and the staff had the freedom to serve people in creative and personalized ways.

On one occasion, the pool staff encountered three teenage boys playing a loud game of volleyball in the adults-only pool. The staff could see that the guests who had chosen the adults-only area for peace and quiet were annoyed. The staff members approached the mother of the teens and explained politely that the resort had two other pools for youngsters. They offered to move her things for her. She pleaded, saying that she liked the cushions on the lounge chairs at the adult pool and did not want to move.

The pool attendants came up with a solution on the spot: They carried the chair cushions across the street to one of the other pools, along with the family's things, and they bought the mother and her family a round of drinks. The next morning, the cushions were waiting for the woman at the family-friendly pool again. A situation that could have ended badly won the pool staff a huge hug, repeat business (the family came back to the SHC the following year), and a raving review on TripAdvisor.

This freedom to act with autonomy applied to the Executive Committee as well. Dale and Stuart gave Matt, Carrie and Adelheid the authority to make decisions big and small. Empowering the SHC's Executive Committee didn't mean Dale and Stuart were out of the loop. On the contrary, they always knew the details of what was going on throughout the organization—one of Dale's mantras was "I don't like surprises." They provided oversight on important matters, and on occasion they had to overrule an Executive Committee member's decision, but they never micromanaged. This balance allowed them to give the Executive Committee and the frontline staff a large degree of freedom, while at the same time ensuring that things never got out of control. This created a spirit of spontaneity and creativity at the SHC, and was one of the main reasons that staff and guests described the culture so often as "authentic."

"When we first visited, we met Heather, the server at the pool, and had an immediate connection," says guest Jeff Seidenfaden. "I am a Platinum Westin member, but when I walk into a Westin I might as well be talking to a parrot. By our second drink at the SHC, Heather already made us want to come back. We told her that we left our dogs at home. She grabbed her phone and showed us a picture of her dog and asked to see a photo of ours. She was engaging and endearing . . . and real."

The amount of thought that went into serving each of the guests astounded me. At times, it even extended beyond the guests staying with us. One afternoon, I was chatting with a woman on property who looked rather frazzled and anxious for a tourist. In fact, she wasn't. She explained to me that she was a Key West local and her entire family was on their way to the hotel from different parts of the U.S. for her brother-in-law's funeral. Her sister and he had lived in the Keys for more than thirty years, and he had suffered a long, painful illness for the past several years. The family was heartbroken and at the same time relieved that he was finally free from pain. They were having dinner that night at the Café, and some of the family were staying at the SHC.

I called Colleen Mulligan, who was the hotel's Guest Relations Manager at the time, to suggest that we send flowers or a card to the family. I should have known she would be ten steps ahead of me. "I have been speaking to the family members for a few days now," she said. "We are buying them dinner, and I have sent his favorite flowers to his wife from us. I also decided to leave cards and flowers in each of the family member's rooms." I had no suggestions to add. "I only wish we could do more," Colleen said.

The majority of the staff at the SHC felt and acted the same way, and they used their decision-making power to care for guests and give them personalized service. Never once in all my time working with the SHC did I see anyone take advantage of that power.

CUT OUT THE RED TAPE

When I began working with the SHC, I quickly discovered that Dale and Stuart rejected most of the tools their competitors used to invert their pyramids. They didn't have an organizational chart, a detailed strategic plan, or policy handbooks—all things my academic training insisted were necessary to run a business efficiently. I tried to get them to adopt these tools, but they politely resisted my suggestions. To them, flexibility

was more important than strict adherence to org charts, protocol, or five-year plans. They knew that what made the SHC
different from its competition was the spirit of authenticity
that came from their staff being empowered and genuinely
engaged. Too much structure and formality, they believed,
would stifle the freedom they had worked so hard to cultivate;
it would spoil everything.

The lack of unnecessary protocol and red tape allowed things
to happen quickly at the SHC. When a manager needed something for a room, a guest or even a staff member, they simply ran
out and got it. If something broke, they got it fixed immediately.
One of the guests at Dewey House relayed this to me in aston-
ishment: "We mentioned to the innkeeper that a handrail next
to the toilet would be helpful. When we got back to our room
later that day, it had been installed. We figured that wouldn't
happen for months!"

In Matt's eyes, this ability to make decisions and act expe-
diently was one of the keys to the SHC's success. "We were able
to give the front lines the authority to do whatever they could
to create a 'wow' experience for the guests, and to make people
feel like they really mattered to us," he recalls.

There was only one set of rules that absolutely could not be
broken, and that was the SHC's code of ethics. One of Dale's most
popular refrains was that we needed to be "beyond reproach."
That meant acting ethically and with integrity in every situation.
Nothing less was acceptable, and staff knew it.

Beyond the code of ethics, Dale and Stuart believed that the
best rule for the SHC was to have as few rules as possible. Stuart
used to tell employees, "I want you act as if you own this hotel."
That could have sounded obnoxious and ironic in a business
where people had no power to act like owners. But at the SHC

the staff were trusted and empowered, and the leaders held an abiding belief that their people had the intellect and good judgment necessary to make the right decisions. Staff appreciated that, and rose to the challenge.

DON'T MAKE POLICIES BASED ON MISTRUST

About fifteen years ago, I was hired by a stand-alone restaurant that had a big problem in the kitchen: They couldn't keep the staff for more than a few weeks. They had earned a bad reputation among hospitality workers in town, and could barely find anyone to apply for a back-of-the-house position. Before I started consulting with the restaurant, I was warned the kitchen manager (who was also part owner of the business) was the reason for the problem. He had installed video cameras in the kitchen, and would spend a good portion of the day remotely watching his employees for mistakes, mishaps and dishonesty. He would then storm into the restaurant and lay into staff for not following a recipe or putting something away improperly or misreading the tickets. When I challenged him about the cameras, he went through a thirty-minute list of examples of all the things he had "caught them doing," including stealing on a few occasions. In his mind, he had no choice but to watch his employees like they were thieves.

More recently, I worked with a restaurant that offered a discount to locals, but would not allow the servers to process the discount. Instead, they would have to find a manager (who might be on a different part of the property) to authorize the discount. Customers appreciated the money off their bill, but not the fifteen-minute wait time to get their check processed. When I asked why servers couldn't do it, the managers pointed out the times a server misused the discount or gave to a non-local in hopes for a better tip. The servers felt inherently mistrusted and frustrated by the need to constantly seek a busy manager.

The problem with creating policies like these is that they are designed to address the bad behaviors of a small minority of employees, but they end up punishing the innocent majority, which kills morale and loyalty.

This isn't to say that people should do whatever they want, whenever they please, and that safeguards should not exist to prevent fraud and theft. At the SHC, inventory was done carefully, re-checked and monitored; cameras were used as a tool for review if an incident occurred (but not as a "Big Brother"); cash-outs were recorded carefully; and time clocks were monitored. These were standard, sensible precautions that could be implemented without overburdening the staff or undermining the culture of empowerment.

"We felt like they trusted us," says Dexter Womble, former Front Desk agent. "They told us all the time that they would trust our decisions and always back us, even if they would have done something different . . . It felt so good to work in an environment where I could do what seemed right without being bound by a million rules and policies."

That trust came with the expectation that it would be repaid with integrity. In the close-knit, family atmosphere of the SHC, people were held to a higher moral standard, even as the leadership team did away with unnecessary rules.

"It wasn't that staff could do whatever they pleased," explains Colleen Mulligan. "There were boundaries, and if we overstepped them, we could be sure we'd be meeting with one of the Executive Committee. The point is that we didn't want to overstep them. We felt grateful for the trust they had in us, and we didn't want to disappoint the customers or them."

INVITE DEBATE

If there is anything Dale doesn't lack, it's confidence. He has strong opinions about most things, and he is not afraid to voice them. Stuart used to muse that even though Dale knows nothing about cooking, he had a habit of telling the chef in the finest restaurants what was missing from their creations. "The interesting thing," Stuart would say laughing, "was that Dale was always right."

While Dale is vociferous about his opinions, he and Stuart both made it a point to seek out the opinions of their staff at the SHC. The two of them spent a good deal of time asking people in meetings and casually in passing for input on every detail of the operation.

Soliciting feedback from their staff wasn't a token gesture. On the contrary, Dale and Stuart knew that the SHC's front lines and managers had a perspective they could never have, and they needed that input to make the business a success. I often sat in meetings in which staff members passionately argued for or against anything from a menu item at happy hour to a new expansion of the hotel. These opinions were not only welcome, they were necessary. If people didn't speak up, Dale and Stuart would ask their thoughts.

This type of discussion is one of the reasons that people feel passionate about an organization. In his best-selling book, *Death by Meetings,* Patrick Lencioni defines a good meeting as one in which stakeholders have a healthy debate about how to make improvements. He argues that a meeting in which people just report is a waste of time, and could be done by email. The key is to use the energy of the people in the room to propel the business forward.

"When there was a controversial issue at hand, we were invited to chime in," recalls Colleen Mulligan. "This meaningful debate made us better stakeholders in decisions that extended beyond our departments . . . Everyone felt that their two cents made a difference."

This approach runs contrary to what I have encountered in other businesses, where I often see managers shut down debate and dismiss the opinions of their staff. One thing I always admired at the SHC was what I would call "contiguous questioning." When someone offered an idea, the entire Executive Committee often asked more questions. Matt would say, "Can you give me an example?" Carrie would ask, "How would that work?" The purpose of these questions wasn't to create the illusion of empowerment; the SHC's leaders actually wanted to dig deeper to understand the point that was being raised.

Seeking input and welcoming healthy debate democratized the information-gathering process at the SHC, as intended, but it didn't mean the organization was managed by consensus. Even as they solicited numerous opinions, Dale and Stuart were 100 percent clear that they or the Executive Committee would be making the final decisions. They used the information to help them understand what people thought and to gather insights from different points of view. The staff understood the process and knew their opinions had been heard, even if their leaders ultimately chose a course of action that was unpopular.

"People can smell crap from a mile away," says longtime staff member Wally Temple. "If they were just asking us our opinion to make us feel good, we would have been over it in no time. They appreciated debate, and they used it to draw their own conclusions. If they didn't agree with us in the end, that was okay. We knew that they took on board what we said."

In so many organizations, the situation is different: Either the staff are not consulted at all when leaders make decisions, or employees bully indecisive leaders into doing what is most popular, not what is best for the business as a whole. Organizations that truly empower their people, like the SHC, must find the middle ground between these two extremes.

A recent study published in the *Harvard Business Review* highlights the importance of leaders allowing for debate within an organization, while still having the flexibility to make autonomous decisions. The 2017 study of more than 17,000 business leaders showed that two-thirds of the most successful CEOs invited debate, but did not default to consensus-driven decision making. Furthermore, the researchers highlight the ability to be decisive as one of the four distinguishing factors of successful leaders.

The way the SHC's leaders made space for people to share their views openly and in depth without the fear of repercussion was a defining characteristic of the culture. It gave people an opportunity to contribute to the decision-making process and made them feel the way Stuart wanted them to: like the business was theirs. At the same time, there was a sense of confidence in the people at the helm, even when the staff preferred different outcomes.

HOW TO EMPOWER YOUR PEOPLE

The success of the SHC is a prime example of how empowering employees leads to a more productive, more engaged, more loyal workforce that provides better service to customers. The challenge in replicating these results comes not from figuring out the right things to say about empowerment, but from actually practicing what you preach. In any industry, and particularly in ones where staff turnover is high and the base compensation rate is not much more than minimum wage, it takes a lot more than talking about how great your work environment is to make employees stay and really care about their jobs; leaders need to actually follow through on the promises they make about empowerment. A select few people happen to have a great work ethic and will bring it to any job, but for the most part, loyalty is earned through actions, not words. People know when the reality of a workplace doesn't match what they hear from leadership. Policies that block creative problem-solving and make innocent people feel guilty foster an "us vs. them" mentality between leaders and front lines, and between front lines and customers. Shutting down debate or asking for input without really listening to what your employees have to say creates mistrust and apathy.

Empowering people is much simpler than the jargon-laden literature on the subject makes it seem: Trust the people you hire and give them as much freedom as you reasonably can to do the job you hired them for, and ask for their opinions about current and future plans for the business as part of the information-gathering phase of your decision-making process.

Here are a few ways you can genuinely empower your employees:

1. *Understand how your people see the business and its culture.* If you really want to know what people think, you have to ask them—and you have to listen to what they tell you. If you get a vague answer, ask again. Don't assume you know what people think. Ask for opinions in meetings; ask people individually; talk to employees at all levels of your organization, from frontline staff to managers to executive leadership. Find out if people feel they have the ability to make decisions and do their jobs without having their hands tied. It is also useful annually to do an anonymous staff survey in which questions about leadership are asked specifically.

2. *Review all your policies that prevent staff from making decisions freely, and eliminate any that are not absolutely necessary.* In this process, ask yourself two questions: "What would we lose if we got rid of this policy or rule?" and "Is this rule or policy made on the assumption that staff are dishonest?" Ask your staff the same questions. The goal is not to eliminate all rules and policies, but to reduce the number to as few as possible.

3. *Tell your people that you want—and actually need—them to make decisions about how best to serve customers.* If you disagree with a decision an employee makes in this capacity, talk to that person about it privately, but still support them. No one should lose their job or feel that they will get in trouble for doing what they think is right for the customer. If they don't believe that you trust in their integrity and have confidence in their ability to make good decisions, they won't use the freedom that is given to them.

4. *Let people debate with you and each other over decisions that would improve the organization.* The more input you get, the better. Ultimately, the leader will make the decision, but shutting opinions down is a surefire way to lose employee engagement. Ask your staff what they think about plans and ideas for improving the business; let them make as many choices that impact their jobs as possible; and thank them for their input. It's okay if the debates sometimes get heated (within reason, and as long as the discussion remains respectful and productive). Passion breeds commitment.

PRINCIPLE 3:
ACCOUNTABILITY

Empowerment without accountability leads to an environment where staff are allowed to do whatever they please, make their own rules, and avoid consequences. When this happens, a business falls apart.

Accountability means that leaders communicate their expectations clearly, and then follow through with rewards and consequences designed to ensure that staff are consistently doing what is expected of them. It sounds simple, but I have found that organizations rarely have effective systems of accountability in place. Too often leaders and managers establish a new policy and then do nothing to hold people accountable for doing and not doing it. They get busy and things just fall through the cracks; or they aren't comfortable with confrontation.

Not long ago I was hired by a big restaurant to help improve leadership and customer service. The investors were impatient with the owner because the restaurant hadn't turned a profit in the two years since it opened, and a new general manager had been brought in to fix the problem. The GM and I met during what should have been a busy lunch hour. The dining room was mostly empty. While the restaurant itself was stunning, they just could not drum up business.

The manager sat across from me at a table in the back, her shoulders slumped. With few customers to serve, her staff had little to do but straighten the table settings and watch the clock. She looked defeated. "I'm spent," she said. Her staff were regularly pulling no-shows, and new hires were leaving for better options after just a few days' work.

When I talked with frontline staff, it was easy to see why. One server summed it up perfectly: "This place is the Wild West. There are no rules, no systems, and everyone gets away with everything."

In my work with businesses of all kinds, I see this kind of problem more often than I can say. Many businesses have great products, but they can't seem to get all the parts of their organization working in sync. There are usually a multitude of reasons for this, but somewhere in the equation is a glaring lack of accountability.

A culture of accountability is based on four key practices: communicating directives clearly; following up on those directives to ensure that staff are doing what is expected; rewarding staff who do what is asked; and providing consequences and taking corrective action when staff are not doing what is asked.

Leaders must be consistent in applying all of these practices. If one or more is missing or not consistently applied, then you have an accountability problem that is undermining your culture and your profitability.

The SHC under Dale and Stuart's leadership is where I saw accountability at its best, and I now teach their practices to all of my clients. As with everything in business, it started at the top. Dale and Stuart placed a high premium on accountability. When Dale issued a directive, it was crystal clear what he expected to be done, and he made sure it was communicated to everyone who needed to know. He would then circle back to make sure that the correct actions were being taken. He would continue to monitor until he knew things were being done as expected on a regular basis. The Executive Committee did the same. The goal wasn't to micromanage, but to establish the crucial elements of accountability. The staff knew what was expected of them, they knew there would be follow-up, and they knew the SHC's leaders would hold them accountable if something wasn't being done right.

It took a lot of effort at first, but once these expectations became the norm, Dale and Stuart and their leadership team could be more strategic in how and when they followed up on their directives. Either they would concentrate on major items of concern, or on staff whom they knew had difficulty being consistent.

I remember one day Dale looked in on the maintenance work area on the property and found it in disarray. Dale wasn't pleased. While the maintenance manager was a loyal and hardworking employee, organizational skills were his challenge. Dale went straight to the maintenance manager's office. He made it clear that the manager and his staff needed to clean up the space and keep it organized. Two days later, Dale checked the area again. Sure enough, it was tidy. But Dale knew it would take consistent follow-up to ensure that the maintenance manager and his team got in the habit of keeping their work area clean, so he came back two weeks later, then a month, then two months. One of those times the work area was in disarray again. I happened to be in the office with the maintenance manager when Dale arrived to address the issue. "You're responsible for this not once, but always," Dale explained. "I will continue to check regularly to make sure we are on task." The maintenance manager apologized. After that, the work area was never a mess again. Whenever Dale saw it neat and clean, he made a point of acknowledging the manager and thanking him.

On another occasion when Dale visited the property, he felt that the grounds looked sloppy. Trash wasn't picked up, hedges were not trimmed neatly, and fences were scuffed. He made sure that every staff member got involved in cleaning up any debris or garbage. He communicated this expectation in a meeting, and made it a habit to inspect the entire property every time he visited. I often saw him walk around and thank his people for keeping the hotel grounds clean. Of course, guests noticed the results as well: It was common to see the word "immaculate" in the guest surveys.

COMMUNICATE EXPECTATIONS CLEARLY

People can't be held accountable for their actions unless they understand expectations in the first place. That's why accountability begins with leaders giving clear and precise directions, and communicating those directives repeatedly to staff in many different ways.

In the late 1990s, the commissioner of the Internal Revenue Service, Charles O. Rossotti, made sweeping changes to redesign systems used by more than 100,000 employees. Before rolling out the changes, IRS leadership created a comprehensive communications program to accompany the process that included training for all staff, videos, internal newsletters, and town hall meetings. The face-to-face meetings received particularly high reviews from staff when they were polled. The end result was a dramatic improvement in the agency's customer satisfaction ratings, which went from an all-time low to the highest in history. The lesson from the IRS is that leaders can't over-communicate when it comes to expressing expectations. The example illustrates the power of sharing information in a multitude of ways so that people receive it many times in multiple forms. One of my mentors, the director of the Peace Corps, in which I volunteered for two years, used to say, "Throw a lot of stones and throw them many times because you never know which one will be a hit."

The SHC obviously didn't operate on the same scale as the IRS, but with a 24/7 operation, more than 250 employees, more than fifteen departments, and a property that spanned two blocks, it would have been easy for communication to break down. And yet, under Dale and Stuart's leadership, there was rarely any confusion regarding the directives coming from the Executive Committee to the front lines. I was always surprised by this—especially since many employees didn't even have email. Nevertheless, everyone seemed to understand what was going on and what their responsibilities were.

Part of this was due to the fact that the leaders of the SHC always followed the same "3 W's" formula for introducing new directives. The formula is simple: They explained what they wanted done, when or how often they wanted it done, and why they were asking that it be done. All directives were communicated to staff in writing (memo, email), and important directives were also communicated in person at staff meetings or one on one.

When a particular request was time-consuming, or required a change of habit, the "Why" component was essential. People often resist change, and they tend to revert back to natural comfort. Hearing the rationale behind a change helped the staff understand the decision and resulted in buy-in.

For example, when Matt decided he wanted the pool attendants to walk guests to their chairs and roll out their towels for them (instead of simply handing guests their towels at the pool entrance), he met with the team in person to explain the change. At first the attendants objected to what he was asking. They were more comfortable handing out towels when guests arrived. The new procedure seemed pushy, and one longtime attendant pointed out that some of the guests didn't want to be fussed over. Matt acknowledged the point, and went on to explain that he thought the new service would make guests feel pampered. The rationale made sense to the pool attendants, and because Matt took the time to communicate it, they dropped their objections.

In addition to using the 3 W's formula, the SHC's leaders focused on communicating clearly and consistently across the organization. They knew it was important that the staff always receive the same message from every member of the Executive Committee. This eliminated much of the confusion that can creep into an organization when its leaders give mixed messages or contradict each other. "I think our greatest strength as a leadership team was our ability to communicate clearly and consistently," says Adelheid Salas, the SHC's Operations Manager. "That made our staff trust us. It gave them confidence in their leaders."

The famous IRS example highlights the importance not only of being clear in communication, but also of using different methods of delivery. A bureaucracy like that could not rely solely on memos and emails; the leaders understood that they needed to share information in a multitude of ways, including in person.

Similarly, Dale and Stuart knew that in-person meetings were an important way to create consistent channels of communication throughout an organization, whether it was amongst management personnel or between management and frontline staff. Meetings ensured that everyone was on the same page at the same time, which helped to eliminate mistakes and oversights. As Food and Beverage Manager Damian DeAngelis recalls, "We spent a lot of time in meetings, but we always left them knowing exactly which part of the project was ours and when it had to get done. It made us all accountable."

Meetings also provided an opportunity for the leaders to gauge people's reactions to new directives, and to connect directly with staff at all levels. They understood that even in this age of e-communication, nothing can take the place of personal interaction. As Dale puts it, "I need to see people's faces when we are communicating. How could we have a real dialogue without it?" He watched people's reactions very closely when he spoke during meetings. If someone seemed confused or frustrated, he would open up the floor for discussion. This simple tactic often cleared up misunderstandings and assuaged concerns on the spot.

The "3 W's" and a consistent focus on communication formed the foundation of accountability at the SHC. Together, these practices enabled the Executive Committee to have confidence that their directives were understood, and that everyone knew what was expected.

FOLLOW UP ON WHAT YOU ASK: SYSTEMS, CHECKLISTS AND THE FEEDBACK LOOP

After creating clear directives and communicating them effectively to your staff, the next step in creating a culture of accountability is following up to make sure things are consistently executed as per your expectations. And yet, many managers and leaders don't establish this habit with their staff because they feel they shouldn't have to. The SHC taught me three simple tools that make it easy to consistently follow up on directives: systems, checklists and feedback loops. Any or all of these can help you ensure that staff stay on track and do what is asked of them on a consistent basis.

For many years I have coached a regional manager of a Fortune 500 global technology and printing company from the East Coast. He brings me to Atlanta every year to their annual meeting to do some training and team-building for the thirty-plus salespeople he manages. His sales force has a taxing job. They manage clients in at least three states and travel constantly. Burnout and turnover are high. It seems I meet an almost entirely new crew every year.

Prior to our last meeting, he complained to me over the phone about "kids today. I send out emails with specific directions every week on what I need from them in their reports, and they act like they never got the instructions," he said. "Some of them don't send me anything for weeks. I feel like I'm dealing with a bunch of fourth-graders."

My client is dealing with a challenge so many managers face. It's tempting to believe that communicating clearly is enough, and that people will do what they are asked simply because they are intrinsically motivated to do their jobs well. For some staff that is the case, and they do their work without the need for follow-up. For others, however, directions can seem more like a suggestion than a mandate.

In a perfect world, a manager would just fire the "fourth graders"; but in many industries, the labor pool does not afford leaders that opportunity. Good hiring practices help (get your

"A Team" on board), but even this doesn't entirely prevent the problem. The bottom line is, you can't create a culture of account- ability without at least some level of follow-up.

The answer is not to be there 24/7 watching over people. In an industry like my client's, and in most industries, that would be impossible. But even if everyone works under the same roof, micromanaging every detail all the time is neither sustainable nor desirable, since it fosters an atmosphere of mistrust and stress.

The solution is to establish a system of consistent and strategic follow-up. That means checking at key moments, and doing it regularly to create a pattern so that staff understand they will be held accountable for what you have asked.

My client and I developed a rotating system in which he reached out (on the phone or by FaceTime) to two of his sales- people daily to "inspect what he expected." He would check in on their activities for that day, and also on specific tasks he had asked them to complete. He'd ask for a progress report on their paperwork, and confirm deadlines for when they would have it completed. Then he left them alone until the due date. If he didn't receive the paperwork on time, sure enough, the person would get a call.

It was a simple system, and it worked. His staff quickly learned that there would be consistent follow-up on progress and dead- lines, and that made them pull through.

The easiest way to establish a pattern of consistent follow-ups is to begin by focusing on one task or directive. I tell my clients to pick the thing that bothers them the most when it doesn't get done consistently. Confirm that your staff understand the directive and what is expected of them, then choose a time frame and stick to it. With regular follow-ups and feedback, the task should begin rolling smoothly. When this happens, move on to another task and repeat the process. Over a relatively short period of time, this pattern of following up becomes a clear expectation. Staff members get the message, and it starts to build a culture in which people know that they will be held accountable.

The Executive Committee at the SHC did this well. They were very detail oriented and circled back with staff on things big and small to make sure that directives were carried out consistently and properly. At the same time, they were very careful not to micromanage.

"Dale refused to micromanage his people," says his wife, Robyn. "He knew the details, and followed up all the time, but he believed that micromanaging was a waste of time."

For example, when Dale wanted staff at the Café to put down coasters under every drink (which they often neglected to do), he made his expectations clear in a meeting, and then came in every few days for a couple of weeks at different times of the day. If he saw even one drink without a coaster under it, he would immediately address the issue and remind the staff of what they were expected to do. He continued to follow up on this until putting down coasters under drinks became automatic for everyone at the Café.

Similarly, when Matt asked the pool attendants to walk guests to their chairs and roll out their towels, he checked in regularly for the first few weeks to monitor the new practice. He made follow-ups like this part of his schedule. For any change in a department, I would see him jot it down in his calendar. He used these notes to remind himself to inspect what he expected. "Matt is very watchful," explains Reservations Manager Barbara Seaman. "He always knew exactly what was going on. He walked the property all the time and noticed if people were following through on big and small things that were asked of them."

When managers followed up on directives at the SHC, they did it respectfully; they didn't embarrass staff. They inquired why things were not getting done, asked for correction, and made sure to circle back again later for another round of follow-up. More importantly, they did what they asked their staff to do and followed their own directives. I often saw Matt, Carrie, and Adelheid handling the Front Desk, helping staff carry luggage, and talking with guests if there was a problem.

"They (the Executive Committee) would pick up garbage off the ground," says Shores Bartender, Megan Ossont. "They were here for events. They came in on the weekends. They used the systems and tools they wanted us to use. Nothing was beneath our leaders, and it made us realize that we had to do the same, plus some."

For the most part, follow-up at the SHC was done informally; but when any department or individual started to slip in performance, the Executive Committee used a simple tool that fixed the problem. Each Department Manager was asked to create a detailed checklist of the major duties the staff was expected to perform. The checklist included both technical duties and customer service principles. If there was a persistent problem with performance, a manager would be asked to observe individual staff members at work every week and complete the checklist for a couple of weeks or even months at a time, depending on the situation. At the end of the employee's shift, the manager would sit down with the individual to review what that person did well and how s/he could improve.

The checklists allowed managers to observe and tweak their staff's performance without having to stand over them every second of every day. Managers were able to give individuals precise feedback to help them get better at their jobs. And there was an additional level of accountability: The checklist forms were submitted to Matt every week, so the management team was held accountable for making sure they were done.

My introduction to the checklists came about a year after I began working with the SHC. There had been a lot of construction for a renovation project, and the disruption was starting to take a toll on the hotel's employees. Guests were complaining frequently about the noise to the Front Desk staff, who were struggling to handle all the complaints courteously and professionally. In addition, we had hired three new people who were not the strongest in their communication skills. Guests started complaining to management about the attitude of the Front Desk staff, and the department's Customer Satisfaction scores in guest surveys plummeted.

Adelheid and her Operations team started to use the checklists, and we saw a turnaround within weeks. We observed every staff member and provided feedback to honor positive performance, and help tweak what was ineffective. Survey scores escalated to near perfection, and the ship sailed smoothly again.

"The checklists meant that staff knew they would be observed on a regular basis," explains Adelheid. "That helped us know what needed work, but it also helped the staff understand that they had to be consistent."

I have used checklists with almost all of my clients since then. Soon after I left the SHC, I took on another hotel that was struggling. At the time, they had been stuck at a ranking of 13 out of 49 on TripAdvisor for two years. The staff were good at the technical and procedural aspects of their jobs, but they never rated better than average on Customer Satisfaction surveys. The General Manager and I created a checklist similar to what was used at the SHC, with a focus on connecting with guests and making them feel special. The GM did checklist observations weekly and sent the results to the hotel's owners. The staff didn't love the idea at first, but in the end, they seemed to appreciate that someone cared enough to observe how they were doing their jobs and provide feedback, including positive feedback for a job well done. In less than two months, the checklists and the new customer-service focus began to make a difference: The hotel moved up to its all-time high on TripAdvisor, and achieved its goal of being in the top 10.

In addition to the checklists, there was another system the SHC's Executive Committee put in place to follow up on guest feedback. The Guest Relations Manager served as the focal point of this process, which I called "The Feedback Loop." Every day the Guest Relations Manager was responsible for scouring social media sites and reading every new guest comment about the resort. She would forward comments (good and bad) to the appropriate department manager. It was then the department manager's job to respond with an explanation of what had been done to address the comment. The process ensured not only that the guest feedback had been received, but that there had been follow-through. If, for example, there was a negative comment about a particular staff member, the department manager would send an email explaining how the information had been shared with the individual, and detailing what further steps, if any, were necessary to help the individual do better in the future.

To ensure accountability at the management level, the Executive Committee was copied on all Feedback Loop com-munications. Dale, Stuart, and the Guest Relations Manager reviewed these messages daily. If a department manager did not respond promptly, he or she would get another email ask-ing for follow-up. This kept the process moving and prevented communication breakdowns. If the guest feedback had only flowed one way, it would have been impossible for the leaders to know if it ever reached the people who needed to hear it. The fact that the manager was held accountable to get back to the Guest Relations Manager ensured that action had been taken.

"Our system for handling guest reviews made a big impact," says Stuart. "The information, good or bad, went directly to individual employees. We followed up very closely and expected a response back."

Creating an effective system for following up with your staff doesn't have to be complicated, but it does take effort on your part. You need to establish the expectation among your staff that their performance will be monitored consistently. When I coach leaders on the principle of accountability, we spend a lot of time on part of the practice. Yes, setting up feedback loops and checklists and making time for regular follow-ups with your staff can be challenging at first, but it always pays off in the long run.

If, as Dale often said, the Devil is in the details, then it's the follow-up on those details that can make or break a business.

MEANINGFUL REWARDS

In my seminars on accountability, I always introduce the topic of rewards under the heading "Consequences." It's a loaded word, and without fail a few people in the audience grimace or shift uncomfortably in their chairs in response. I've had participants tell me that it conjures up images of dour Catholic School nuns slapping knuckles with wooden rulers.

I find it interesting that consequences are associated most often with punishment and discipline, rather than with rewards, when in fact a consequence is simply what happens as a result of a particular action. In management, it's important to always keep the full definition in mind. Managers and leaders need to make sure that people are acknowledged for what they do well, not just reprimanded when they falter. Indeed, *reward* is the desired destination on the accountability train. It is the result of the effort that people put in to consistently doing their jobs well, and it perpetuates more of the same right action.

For most of us, it feels great to thank someone, give a gift, or share a compliment we overheard about them, but I rarely see managers do this well on a consistent basis. Some leaders I coach are overly reliant on their organization's systems of rewards, like the Timex an employee receives after five years of service or Employee of the Month certificates. These things are nice, but when everyone gets the same generic, institutionalized rewards, the rewards lose their power to make people feel appreciated.

Worse, some leaders think rewarding their employees is a bunch of touchy-feely nonsense. More than one client has challenged the idea with a variation of the line, "Why do I have to thank my people all the time? I pay them to do a job."

When leaders adopt this defiant attitude, they are missing a fundamental truth about human nature that ultimately costs them money, morale, and time. Research proves that a lack of acknowledgment and appreciation has a direct impact on job performance, and ultimately on an organization's bottom line. A recent study by KPMG, one of the four biggest professional services companies worldwide, shows that businesses that effectively recognize excellence enjoy a Return on Equity (ROE) more than three times higher than firms that do not. Despite these astounding figures, many leaders still don't make an effort to reward a job well done: A recent Gallup Poll study showed that 65 percent of Americans received no praise or recognition in the workplace in the past year.

The Executive Committee at the SHC knew the importance of rewarding their staff, and they knew how to deliver those gifts meaningfully. These efforts led to a more engaged, loyal, and happier workforce. "Acknowledging and thanking people is more important than anything," says Stuart. "It appeals to one's sense of self-worth, and makes us all feel a part of something."

The leaders at the SHC embraced the typical systems practiced by most businesses. They had Employee of the Month and Employee of the Year programs, gifts for years of service, and annual bonuses. Every year they threw a great Employee Appreciation and holiday party. But these institutionalized programs and events were only about 10 percent of what the Executive Committee did to acknowledge and inspire their staff. The rest of their efforts were made up of two other forms of rewards—meaningful praise and personalized gifts.

As they walked around the property daily, the Executive Committee made it a point to tell the frontline staff what they were doing well, and how important their efforts were. Carrie was a master at this skill. Whether it was helping someone with their luggage, making a family laugh around the pool, or a small act of kindness for a guest or co-worker, she seemed to notice all the good things people were doing, and she never missed an opportunity to acknowledge them. "Carrie was always in tune with what our staff members cared about," recalls Adelheid. "She was so good at thanking people in ways that really made them feel special."

The praise Carrie offered was simple yet meaningful. The staff knew she was watching, and they respected her so much that they wanted to please her. Plus, it felt good to them to help others in the way that their bosses helped them.

Stuart had his own special way of making the staff feel like they were valued. The frontline employees often told me stories of how he had gone out of his way to compliment them and thank them personally for something they had done. His gratitude and praise were so genuine that people knew it came from close observation, and from the heart.

"Stuart used to tell me how great I was with people and that I was gifted at it," says Shores Bar server Kelly. "In fact, he told me I was too good at people skills to be a waitress! How many bosses would say something like that? They would try to keep the people who did well for them at all costs. I could see how much he valued what I did. It made me want to keep doing well for him and the guests."

When a great TripAdvisor review mentioned an employee by name, Matt would write the person a personalized note of appreciation and search the property to hand it to him/her directly. I didn't realize how meaningful these notes were until I was talking with a member of the maintenance staff at an annual employee party, and he pulled out of his wallet a note Matt had written, thanking him for a job well done. He proudly showed me the note. The paper looked tattered around the edges, like it had been in his wallet for a long time.

"Did you just bring that to the party, or do you always keep that on you?" I asked.

He laughed. "I keep it to remind me on a tough day that I do a great job in my boss' eyes."

What surprised me even more than the fact that this tough guy carried around an accolade in his wallet, was that his boss' opinion of him meant so much. It seems to me that most people don't respect their bosses enough to care much what they think, let alone to have their words impact them so deeply. But in the SHC's culture, the leaders earned their staff's respect through their care and watchful attention to their staff's actions. To the large majority, their leaders' opinions of them meant a great deal.

From my observation, the simple act of noticing what the staff did well and acknowledging it specifically and authentically was the number one thing the leaders of the SHC did to inspire great morale. And the rewards didn't stop at praise. The Executive Committee found unexpected ways to personalize gifts for individuals and teams to thank them—things like spontaneously bringing in breakfast for the staff on a busy morning, and taking an employee out to a surprise lunch at their favorite restaurant on their birthday. The personal touches mattered as much as the gifts themselves, because they were yet another reminder that the SHC's leaders genuinely valued their employees as people.

The personalized gifts were usually small but significant things. For example, Adelheid once overheard the Front Desk staff talking about wanting to try a great new Cuban restaurant that had recently opened on the island. She made a mental note, and during "Hell Week" (the busiest week of the year for tourism in Key West, between Christmas and the New Year) she had lunch catered for them from the new restaurant to thank them.

Sometimes, the SHC's leaders took advantage of spontaneous opportunities to thank their people not for anything in particular, but for their ongoing efforts.

"One night we were out to dinner," recalls Stuart's wife, Susan. "We saw a group of bartenders having dinner at the same restaurant. They were great employees, always going above and beyond for the guests. We asked the server to give us the bill. We tried to do unexpected things like that as often as we could."

These personalized, unexpected acts of kindness endeared the leaders to their staff, and made them feel like family.

"Susan was so loving and down to Earth. She and Stuart were like our grandparents," says Property Manager, Todd Jones. "They became mentors to us, and we knew we mattered to them."

Not surprisingly, these random acts of appreciation inspired the staff to do the same with guests.

"The way they (the leaders) gave to us (the staff) made us become more proactive with our guests," says former Guest Relations Manager Colleen Mulligan. "We looked for ways to surprise our customers and give them even more than they were expecting."

The leaders of the SHC elevated the practice of rewarding and recognizing their employees to an art form. They made sure that the consequences that followed from someone's hard work and dedication were always positive, and in doing so, they encouraged more of the same. The rewards and recognition they bestowed upon the staff weren't seen by the leaders as a chore, or as fluff, but as something significant and meaningful. They understood that people need to feel they are "part of something," as Stuart once said, and need to be acknowledged for what they contribute. Above all, they knew that rewarding their staff would help to reinforce the SHC's culture of accountability.

REMEDIATION: ON-THE-SPOT CORRECTION AND SKILLS TRAINING

Rewards are the fun part of the accountability equation. But what happens when staff members aren't following through on your directives consistently? That's where remediation comes in. Giving negative feedback and having awkward conversations about how an employee needs to improve his or her performance isn't fun, but if you don't actively remediate performance problems, you can't create a culture of accountability. On the flip side, if you do this well, you will discover that many employees appreciate the feedback because they want to know when they are doing something wrong and how they can improve.

I recently facilitated a mediation between a longtime employee and her manager. They sat across from each other, avoiding eye contact and trying to hide behind their steaming coffee cups. The employee was a server at an upscale restaurant, and she had worked there since it opened. But at the end of her shift the night before we met, she had submitted her resignation with no explanation. When her manager asked why, she said she felt disliked by him and the other staff.

After listening to her in our mediation, the manager acknowledged his part of it, and admitted that indeed he was frustrated with certain aspects of her performance. He then went on to list the tasks she had not been doing well for many months: She made mistakes in the computer system, didn't do her side work adequately, and expressed her disapproval with management decisions openly.

She was shocked to hear all this. "Why didn't you tell me?" she asked.

The manager answered bluntly: "It wouldn't result in anything."

"Don't you think I deserve the opportunity to get better?" she asked, clearly wounded by his response.

There was no need for me to interject. He sat there quietly for a few moments, then said, "Of course. I should have come to you sooner."

Immediately after the meeting ended, the manager asked me if we could talk. He confided in me that he knows he can be harsh, and for that reason he often chooses not to give his employees any feedback at all. The server's question was a wake-up call: He had realized that failing to give feedback when staff were not performing was more detrimental than any mistake the staff could make. His displeasure with them would be palpable, and the lack of communication could only make matters worse—far worse, in fact—than telling them directly what was wrong.

From the outside it's easy to see the manager's mistake, and yet when we are in his shoes, we are often tempted to do the same. Most of us are guilty of avoiding confrontation, even when it is necessary to resolve an issue. We fear that our attempts to correct the situation will be met with defiance, or that we won't handle the confrontation well, or that nothing will change even if we address the issue head-on. So we convince ourselves that we're better off doing nothing, and we hope the issue will somehow resolve itself.

That is a monumental mistake. The number one failure I see in relationships, both personal and professional, is an unwillingness or inability to confront issues. When problems aren't confronted and directly addressed, they fester and grow more serious. It is like living with a low-grade infection and not doing anything to treat it. Eventually the infection gets worse, and by the time it gets the needed attention, it may be too late. As a leader, you can't let this happen in your organization.

At the SHC, the Executive Committee was as active in correcting mistakes as they were in giving praise and rewards. They remediated through two key interventions that were simple yet very effective: on-the-spot correction and skills training. They tried these two actions consistently before resorting to disciplinary action, which is the path most organizations rely on for correcting behavior.

"We were constantly striving for perfection," says Dale. "That didn't mean anyone got punished when we didn't get there. I always explained to people what we did well, and when I saw something we could do better, I told them just as quickly. Then we worked on solutions."

Stuart did the same. "I felt it was my role to call attention to things that weren't right just as much as I did to the things that were," he says. "It was our job to be the reinforcers."

When Adelheid observed a problem with how the Front Desk staff were serving guests, she would take the earliest opportunity to provide direct and clear feedback about how she expected the situation to be handled in the future. There was no sugarcoating of the criticism, but there was no belittling of employees either. Adelheid simply explained what had been done wrong, and what needed to be done differently. The next time she witnessed the interaction done well, she was sure to acknowledge the staff members with praise. And if anyone needed support to improve their performance, she was there to help, no questions asked.

Matt and Carrie had a similar style. If they saw a staff member doing something wrong, they would take the individual aside to address the issue immediately, if possible. They always did this quietly, respectfully, and succinctly. It was a simple technique that functioned as a form of daily, on-the-spot training. Most of the time the staff appreciated the feedback.

"I enjoyed the support I got when I was learning the front desk," says Mulligan. "If I did something wrong, I was corrected in a positive way and reassured that I could and should ask for help if I needed it. I felt like I had all the tools and consistent feedback I needed. They knew what we did well, and what we needed to improve."

On-the-spot correction was only part of the remediation process at the SHC. If an employee received several on-the-spot corrections and continued to struggle, managers had two other options for addressing the situation. The first option was to have the employee go through skills coaching, which I would design around the person's specific weaknesses. The second option was a more formal disciplinary process similar to what is typical in most organizations, beginning with a write-up, then a suspension, and culminating in termination, if necessary. Managers used the first option whenever possible. The goal wasn't to punish people for making mistakes; it was to help them do better in the future.

Most of the time a combination of on-the-spot correction and formalized skills training worked to resolve the issue. In cases where the disciplinary process began, it was often used alongside the skills training, as happened with a very skilled and talented maintenance staff member who started having problems with his co-workers. The Maintenance Manager sat him down and explained the need to be more respectful and more of a team player. Things improved for a few days, but soon the problem returned. At that point, the manager asked me to do three coaching sessions on communication with him while, at the same time, putting the employee on the disciplinary path with a write-up. The write-up made it clear to the employee that the situation was unacceptable, and that his job was at risk if he didn't change his behavior. The skills coaching made it clear that his manager genuinely wanted him to correct the problem, and was giving him the opportunity to do it.

The remediation process at the SHC proved to be extremely effective. It assured the staff that while the expectations were high, they would be given the support and the tools they needed to meet those expectations. Instead of simply saying "You did something wrong and we need you to change," managers and the Executive Committee were able to help their talented people learn new skills and improve on their weaknesses. It didn't work in every case, and, like all organizations, the SHC sometimes had to part ways with employees who couldn't or wouldn't do what was required of them; yet even these individuals knew the SHC's leaders had tried to make it work. The Executive Committee wasn't shy about using progressive discipline when necessary, but it wasn't the first step in accountability. They worked with each individual as best they could before going down the path of separation. And on the occasions they chose that path, they were decisive about it. They didn't prolong the process with ten write-ups and half-hearted disciplinary meetings. When it was time to part ways with an employee, they did it. Their decisiveness sent a message to the staff that while everyone would be given tools and a chance to improve, no one would be allowed to take advantage of those tools or the people who offered them.

In the end, it's easy to lose sight of the fact that remediation doesn't only involve punishment, just as it's easy to forget that consequences can be positive and negative. Leaders who want to create a culture of accountability in their organization must deal with problems directly head-on, and be able to address performance issues in a positive way. No one likes confrontation, even when it's handled effectively, but avoiding it only causes more problems in the long run.

CREATING ACCOUNTABILITY IN YOUR ORGANIZATION

When I begin working with clients who are struggling with a lack of accountability in their organizations, one of the common complaints I hear is, *No one follows directions.* This always reminds me of the tired restaurant manager with the defeated look in her eyes, who described the culture of her restaurant as the Wild West.

In other cases, I see the opposite: leaders who are micromanagers or fearmongers. While no one in these organizations would dare show up late, staff morale is in the tubes. When that leader is not present, all hell breaks loose, and turnover is high.

Both of these leadership styles yield the same result: a lack of genuine desire on the part of staff to do what is being asked of them to the best of their abilities.

Creating accountability in an organization requires a delicate balancing act. Accountability comes when leaders consistently provide the following to their staff: clear directives, effective communication and follow-up, and consequences—rewards for a job well done, and corrective action to improve performance.

To establish or improve systems of accountability in your department or organization, try the following:

1. *Give clear and consistent directives to your staff.* Explain in no uncertain terms what you expect them to do, when you want it done, and why you want it done that way—that's the "3 W's." Communicate your directives multiple times and via multiple channels (memo, email, in person), and make sure people understand what is expected. After giving a directive, ask "What's the plan?" (This is especially effective when there is a language barrier.) If the individuals receiving the directive are able to repeat back the What, When, and Why of it, you know you can be confident that everyone is on the same page.

2. *Follow up regularly and consistently on your directives.* This isn't a call to micromanage your employees, but it is important to regularly observe how they are performing their duties to ensure that your directives are being followed. When you ask for a specific task to be done, put it in your calendar as a reminder on a weekly or bi-weekly basis to check in and see how it is going. Involve your supervisors and middle managers in the follow-up process. If individuals or departments are having trouble consistently following a directive, have your

managers do weekly observation checklists as a way of providing direct feedback on individual performance. Establish a system for collecting customer feedback, and pay close attention. Your customers will tell you better than anyone whether your directives are being followed. Make sure that the feedback from your customers gets to frontline staff by designating a point person to manage the delivery of that information and create a feedback loop.

3. **Make sure there are consequences for doing or not doing what you ask.** Consequences involve both *rewards* and *remediation*. Rewards are important because staff must know that they will be acknowledged for a job well done. You can do this with verbal or written praise, and with personalized rewards that let people know you see what they do and you appreciate them as individuals for their efforts. When there are performance issues, address the problem directly. Remediation can take the form of on-the-spot correction, formal training, or disciplinary action. I usually advise my clients to use the Socratic method for on-the-spot correction. Questions like "Why didn't this happen?" "What would it take to make it happen?" and "When can it get done?" are effective at framing the correction as a conversation, rather than a punishment, and they encourage people to take ownership of the problem and the solution. When on-the-spot correction doesn't work, ask yourself whether the person *can't* or *won't* do what is expected. If it's the former, spend time coaching that individual to give him/her tools to accomplish the task. If it's the latter, be prepared to take disciplinary action, usually beginning with a write-up and, if necessary, culminating in termination.

PRINCIPLE 4:
MANAGE AND RESOLVE STAFF CONFLICTS CONSTRUCTIVELY

STUDIES ON CONFLICT IN THE WORKPLACE show that managers spend up to 80 percent of their time managing customer and employee conflicts. The irony is that most of them never receive any training on how to do it. Over the past twenty-plus years, I've worked with leaders who run the gamut in their approach to managing conflicts—from a Shiite Mukhtar in Iraq who told me that negotiating is a "sign of weakness," to a school principal who believed that being weak was the only way to keep her staff happy. Learning how to resolve conflict effectively requires every tool in the communication toolbox—from active listening to assertiveness and learning how to seek a win-win solution. Doing all of this well requires thought, study and a good deal of trial and error.

As different as Dale and Stuart were in their communication styles, their philosophical approach to resolving conflict was exactly the same: They dealt with the problem head-on, listened thoroughly to everyone involved, got to the bottom of the issue, and always, always looked for concrete solutions. They had boundless energy for getting to the heart of the matter, and they almost never dismissed a conflict as trivial or petty. If it mattered to their customers or staff, it mattered to them. Most importantly, they had a heartfelt belief that almost any conflict could be resolved, if the people at the negotiation table cared enough.

I saw this principle in action from the moment I started working with the SHC. In fact, I was brought in to mediate what I initially believed was an unresolvable conflict between two of the hotel's most important leaders—Matt and Carrie Babich.

On the day I met Matt, I was trying very hard to avoid seeing anyone. I had just returned the night before from a grueling trip to post-war Kosovo, where I had been mediating and teaching conflict-resolution for almost three weeks. Coming back to the warm, lighthearted vibe of Key West had never felt so good.

I was on the beach in front of the Southernmost Beach Café, dizzy from jet lag and hoping a Bloody Mary and some sun would help me unwind, when Matt walked up and introduced himself. I knew him by reputation as the General Manager of the SHC—by that point, everyone in Key West did—and despite his casual polo shirt and shorts, I could tell he was a man on a mission. I was glad I hadn't yet downed my cocktail.

"Sorry to bother you," he said nervously, "but I was just thinking this week of how to contact you." Then, before I could make a polite comment or ask what he wanted to talk about, he cut to the chase: He really, really needed some help, and he needed it fast, but he couldn't explain why at the Café. He said it would be best to talk in private.

"Did you rob a bank?" I joked, hoping to lighten the mood.

"Worse," he said.

A few days later, Matt was sitting in front of me in my office, looking as nervous as he had on the beach. He poured out a story of how he and Carrie had decided to end their nearly twenty-year marriage. The difficult situation was further complicated by the fact that they not only worked together, but essentially co-managed the SHC. While they hadn't made a formal announcement to the staff, a few people at the hotel knew what was happening. The only thing Matt and Carrie could agree on was that they didn't want to work together anymore; each wanted the other out of the picture. The constant tension between them was escalating. The once-great couple who were the face of the SHC could now barely speak to each other.

I offered Matt some options on how he might proceed, and suggested that he think them over and we could talk again in a few days.

Before Matt got back to me, Dale called. He gave me his perspective on the situation, and told me what he and Stuart were going to do about it.

"We're not letting either of them go," he said resolutely. "They are both extremely valuable to the operation, and I need them both. We have to make this work."

Fat chance, I thought. I couldn't imagine how Matt and Carrie could continue to co-lead when they could barely be in the same room together. If they stayed in their respective positions, the ongoing conflict between them would inevitably divide the staff and create turmoil throughout the organization.

Dale confirmed that I wasn't the only one who thought that. He had consulted a respected psychologist in Detroit, who pretty much told him that keeping both Matt and Carrie would be impossible.

But Dale was determined to find a solution. He had changed the SHC's management structure so that Matt and Carrie both reported directly to him, rather than having Carrie report to Matt. This minimized their interactions within the workplace and allowed Dale to give them each distinctly separate responsibilities. He also formed the Executive Committee, which was comprised of Dale, Stuart, Adelheid, Matt and Carrie. The Executive Committee met monthly, and it was the forum within which Matt and Carrie could express their differences of opinion with respect to business matters. Dale was convinced the arrangement would work, but he needed my help.

"As a lawyer, I can help facilitate their divorce," Dale explained. "I want you to mediate their personal issues so that they can work together effectively."

Suddenly, Kosovo was sounding pretty good.

In so many words I told him I thought his idea was crazy. My impression was that all the mediation in the world couldn't salvage the situation.

Dale was undeterred. "I'm asking you to try," he said.

Thus began a three-month process in which I met with Matt and Carrie on a weekly basis (sometimes more often) to mediate their relationship so that they could both lead the organization as they always had. It was difficult and sometimes volatile, and more than once I thought we might have to give up, but Matt and Carrie persevered. They made the professional relationship work, and their staff genuinely still saw them as a team. Dale has often said that keeping both Matt and Carrie on board at the SHC was one of the greatest challenges of his career, as well as one of his proudest accomplishments.

It's also one of the most unconventional business situations I have ever been involved in. Whenever I tell the story, I have to point out that I'm not advising businesses to hire married couples as leaders, or to mediate divorces between employees. But the principles at the heart of the story are more universal: Sticking too closely to absolute, black-and-white policies can be a mistake, and managing challenges that may seem unconventional—or even crazy—can be extremely productive.

The SHC's Executive Committee managed challenging personalities and staff conflicts with remarkable success, and they did it in ways that gave their people every possible chance to succeed. Three things set the SHC apart from other organizations in this regard: the first was a focus on specific, measurable resolutions to conflicts; the second was effectively managing their mavericks; and third was their use of curative coaching and mediation.

FOCUS ON SPECIFIC AND MEASURABLE SOLUTIONS

When it comes to employee conflicts, almost any manager can have a "come to Jesus" conversation in which he/she tells the employee that his or her problem behavior must change. Or if two employees are fighting, that same manager can tell them to "get over it" and require them to get along. Similarly, anyone can offer an apology to an unhappy customer. All of these approaches are well-meaning but largely ineffective, because they are missing the one thing that is absolutely necessary to repair a problem: a solution. And not just any solution will do. If you want to truly resolve a problem, you need to focus on solutions that are specific and measurable.

If the SHC had a manager who was weak, Dale wasn't interested in a general pledge to "do better"; instead he required concrete commitments that specified how the manager was going to improve performance. I saw him push the point hard at times, and he always walked away with an action-based plan. He and Stuart expected their staff to handle customer complaints the same way. It wasn't enough to just apologize to an unhappy guest. The important question was, "What are we going to *do* about it?"

In one case, there was a tough manager who was great at her job, but had a bad habit of alienating her co-workers by being short, curt, and holding grudges. Ironically, she was very sensitive herself, and she often broke down in tears and threatened to quit if anyone tried to address her shortcomings. After hearing this story a number of times, Dale decided it was time to intervene. He had a stern talk with her that ended with him laying out the specific behaviors she needed to change, and the actions she needed to take in order to make those changes (speaking to others in a respectful tone, confronting people privately instead of at staff meetings, listening to what others had to say, and trying harder to accommodate requests). Simply telling her to get along better with her peers would not have been effective. She needed to hear how to do that, and she needed have a concrete action plan in place to help her make the necessary changes.

This approach was music to my ears when I first started working with the SHC. In my own formal training in mediation and conflict-resolution there was great emphasis placed on SMART solutions (Specific, Measurable, Attainable, Realistic and Time-sensitive). I can't count the number of times I have had the conversation with managers about the need for concrete action to resolve conflicts. I often tell people in my seminars, "If you don't walk out of the discussion with specific solutions, you have wasted your time having the talk." No conflict ever got resolved by airing grievances and discussing differences. Talking is just the first step; it must be followed by actions that create lasting change.

At the SHC, staff complaints were generally given as much attention as those of the guests, and taken just as seriously. "If our people were fighting with each other, how could they genuinely provide good service to our guests?" says Stuart. "We didn't sit around and do nothing when a guest was upset. The same was true for our staff."

Often when Dale and Stuart were on property they would get involved in staff issues, big and small. They never thought twice about convening people themselves instead of ordering their mangers to do it. That sent a clear message to the entire organization that problems would not be swept under the carpet. Managers at every level were expected to get involved when there was conflict and make sure it got resolved.

Psychologist and author Harriet B. Braiker, who wrote extensively on the subject of how conflict affects people's personal and professional lives, affirms Dale and Stuart's approach: "Conflict can and should be handled constructively; when it is, relationships benefit. Conflict avoidance is not the hallmark of a good relationship. On the contrary, it is a symptom of serious problems and of poor communication."

Dale and Stuart understood this intuitively because they valued relationships. Getting involved to make sure conflicts got resolved constructively was natural for them, and it was one of the things that helped make relationship such an important part of the culture of the SHC. From the front lines, all the way up to the top, staff knew that they could reach out for help with their conflicts and that someone would not only listen, but work with them to resolve it.

BE FLEXIBLE WITH YOUR MAVERICKS

Every organization has at least a few "mavericks." The term is used frequently by best-selling author, Hans Finkel, in his book *The 10 Mistakes Leaders Make*. Finkel used it to describe high-performing employees who shake things up, push new agendas, and often have quirky habits. Finkel argues that while mavericks and the turmoil they often cause can be challenging to manage, they are actually the lifeblood of an organization.

Effectively managing your mavericks requires a lot of flexibility. Co-workers tend to perceive a maverick's quirks and creativity as rogue behavior. Leaders who think this way tend to take a disciplinary approach to dealing with mavericks. This is a mistake. It sends the message that conformity matters more than what a person contributes professionally and personally to your organization. You need to enforce certain standards of conduct, of course, but you can't create a unique, authentic culture if you expect your people to be robots that all think and act the same. If you are too strict with your mavericks, you risk putting a damper on their creativity, or worse, driving them out of your organization entirely. "Don't allow your policies and procedures to stifle your brightest stars," writes Finkel. "Be flexible. Bend the rules if you believe that someone needs more space. Never be in bondage to your policy manual. Rules are made to be broken, principles are not."

Dale often used a similar refrain at the SHC: "We don't need everyone to be in the same lane. But they have to be on the same road."

A case in point was Duane Webster, the SHC's Information Technology Manager. Duane was originally the IT consultant in Dale and Stuart's offices in Michigan. They were so impressed with his technical knowledge and skills that they periodically brought him to Key West to consult on IT issues at the hotel. When Duane expressed a desire to live in Key West, Dale and Stuart decided that he would be a good addition to the "A Team." As they had done in the past with other great employees, they moved him to Key West and brought him aboard at the SHC. Within a relatively short time, he had created an IT center on property that was light-years beyond what had existed before—and beyond what anyone understood.

Duane began addressing a myriad of issues, including internet, television, computers and property management systems. With such a smart guy on top of things, the staff expected that their computer problems would be solved, but in fact Matt and the Front Desk staff soon found themselves frustrated. They had a long list of projects for Duane, but it seemed to take forever for him to get anything done. Duane's tendency to use highly technical language only added to the frustration. When Matt or his staff questioned Duane about missed deadlines, he would respond in what sounded like defensive gobbledygook. People began to question whether Duane really knew what he was doing.

Dale got wind of the situation and immediately stepped in. He didn't mind mavericks; in fact, he valued them. He understood that it would take some extra effort to help the organization adapt to Duane, and vice versa. He also understood that the results would be worth it. "Duane had technical expertise that no one else on staff had," says Dale. "They could not understand what he was doing, so they made assumptions that he wasn't managing his time well."

Dale asked me to coach Duane to give him tools for multi-tasking. In addition, he gave Duane two assignments: The first was to keep a daily log of how he spent his time for two weeks. The second was to create an itemized task-list for all the projects he had in the pipeline, with corresponding estimates of the time frame required to complete each task. Dale then worked personally with Duane and Matt to establish new deadlines for the projects based on Duane's estimates.

It was a detailed and laborious task, but proved necessary. Over the next few months, the daily log illustrated an accurate depiction of Duane's timeline on tasks and projects. When Dale and Duane compared the logged time to Duane's estimated times, they immediately realized the problem: The work was taking three times longer than Duane projected.

"He had too many projects on his plate, and the time frames in which he was trying to do them were unrealistic," says Dale. In other words, Duane was setting unreachable goals for himself, and no one had taken the time to analyze the root cause of the problem. Instead, people had just assumed the worst—that Duane was undependable and not diligent. Dale and Duane went back to the project list and worked out a solution. "We had to reevaluate priorities and put realistic timelines to each one," says Dale. "Then, we had to give him some additional support to finish the projects on a timely basis."

The result was a clear schedule with priorities that Matt and Duane evaluated together weekly. Almost immediately, the relationship and workflow improved.

Dale's approach with Duane exemplifies how mavericks were managed at the SHC. The goal was to be smart, practical, and flexible, and to keep high-performing but challenging individuals within the organization. The SHC's leaders knew that in most cases, it was well worth the effort.

"We were trying to create a culture that was different and better than any other place," says Dale. "We couldn't expect everyone to automatically fit in. We put time and energy into our people to cultivate that culture of greatness."

CURATIVE COACHING AND MEDIATION

Ask twenty people what coaching and mediation mean and you'll get forty answers. Some managers think coaching is synonymous with a disciplinary talk, while others use it as a euphemism for firing. At the SHC, *curative coaching* referred to the process of working with an employee on a continuous basis to improve performance. It involved specific agreements (usually between three and ten) and required consistent follow-up to ensure accountability.

Mediation is when one individual convenes with two or more parties to reach consensus on a specific issue or problem. The mediator is neutral (even if he or she has an opinion), and does not arbitrate by telling the parties what they should or should not do. It is a highly controlled process that results in specific agreements which, like curative coaching, are monitored on a continuous basis.

During my time with the SHC, mediating conflicts and curative coaching for employees at all levels were two of my primary responsibilities. This meant that the organization had someone on board who was trained to manage conflicts, and who could teach others to do the same. In my mind, this was a game-changer for the SHC. Instead of waiting for a crisis to erupt and then reactively organizing a big venting session, or throwing out a hollow order for everyone to work as a team, I could help staff get down to root causes. I pushed hard to make sure issues were resolved and not just papered over, to give people tools and training that would actually help them, and to oversee follow-up. This put concrete, long-term solutions in place and fixed problems in a meaningful way.

Mediation works for conflicts of all size. It proved effective for helping Matt and Carrie establish a constructive working relationship after their contentious divorce, and it resolved tensions between entire departments.

It is common in hotels for there to be a little tension between the Front Desk and Reservations. Reservations may move a guest at the last minute, leaving the Front Desk to deal with the fallout from the angry customer. Conversely, Front Desk sometimes offers a rate discount to a guest, or may move them to a room Reservations was prepared to sell. When a hotel is at full occupancy during the busy season, or when there are computer problems, the already strained dynamic between the two departments can get ugly.

This happened at the SHC in 2010. The hotel had just made the switch to a new property management system, and there were mixed feelings about it. The Reservations department, which also was in charge of revenue management (setting rates and monitoring bookings), loved the new system because of the detailed reports it could produce. The Front Desk, on the other hand, hated the system because it was difficult to learn and seemed to slow down the check-in process. (Many of the frustrations the Front Desk agents were experiencing had to do with system bugs, which the provider was fixing, but the fixes weren't coming fast enough to prevent the conflict between the departments from escalating.)

Not long after the rollout of the new system, underlying tensions between the Front Desk and Reservations reached an all-time high. The Front Desk department, Matt, and Duane all wanted to abandon the new system and roll back to the old system, while the Reservations department was adamant that the new system be retained.

Dale and Stuart got involved right away and called a meeting of everyone involved to discuss possible courses of action. After listening to all sides of the argument, and following a lot of analysis and several firm discussions with the software provider, Dale and Stuart decided to move forward with the new system. The provider put a full-time person on premises for as long as it took to work out the bugs.

Concurrently, the Executive Committee asked me to mediate between the Front Desk and Reservations. The resentment level was high, and it was negatively affecting morale in other departments, as well. After a series of meetings, the teams from both sides clarified the key problems and developed specific solutions for systems and behaviors that would improve communication. Everyone agreed to the solutions.

I checked in with both departments informally on a weekly basis, and we met monthly for three months so they could score themselves on their improvement on each agreement. The process was detailed and targeted. Things settled down across the board, and everyone unanimously reported improvement.

The agreements in place were what made the mediation work. Instead of being lectured by a manager and ordered to play nice, we got down to the heart of the matter and made changes that were concrete and measurable.

Hiring an outsider to handle mediations didn't mean the SHC leaders farmed out their problems. In fact, part of the process required me to train managers how to mediate conflicts and more effectively coach their staff, and to assist the managers in learning and refining those tools. Over time, some members of the management team became excellent mediators and coaches in their own right, and could do fine without my assistance.

"I think we were able to help a lot of people in the end," says Dale. "We helped solve problems, and also gave our managers skills they could use for a lifetime."

Dale and Stuart also recognized the importance of curative coaching, and how it could be helpful to SHC. They asked me to coach individuals who needed sharper skills, and more importantly, they made sure they communicated to that person that the process was important. Without their support, the coaching wouldn't have been nearly as effective.

As you will recall from the accountability principle, curative coaching at the SHC was about growing people, not punishing them. The staff came to understand this, and after I had been there for a couple of years, employees at all levels began seeking me out to request coaching, without having been sent by their managers. To me, that was proof that coaching had become what it should be at its best—a tool people want, so that they can get better at their jobs and feel happier in their lives.

The key to making both mediation and curative coaching work is surprisingly simple: You have to follow up to make sure the agreements are being upheld by everyone involved. Start with weekly check-in meetings, then transition to monthly check-ins after you have established the expectation that people will be held accountable for following through on specific agreements. When employees know they will have regular check-in meetings, they are far more likely to stick to their agreements.

The check-ins are easy to do. As the leader, you bring the agreements to the meeting in writing. Together with the employee(s), you review each agreement and discuss if they are working or not. I suggest scoring each agreement by giving it a plus or minus to clearly indicate what is going well and what needs improvement.

In my experience, check-in meetings are most effective when they are held once a week for three weeks, and then once per month for three months. After that, the agreements tend to stick. If they don't, the next step is progressive discipline.

Curative coaching and mediation should always precede disciplinary action, and they must be tied to specific behavioral changes. If you are committed to keeping great people and helping individuals improve their performance, these are critical leadership skills to develop.

HOW TO EFFECTIVELY RESOLVE CONFLICTS IN YOUR ORGANIZATION

Every organization must contend with difficult people and staff conflicts. It is a simple fact of life, and yet these people and their problems are often seen as a burden, rather than an opportunity. Emotional Equity is about recognizing the opportunities. Leaders must be willing and able to get involved and manage conflicts to arrive at constructive resolutions. This requires more than inspirational talks. It means valuing relationships. It means being flexible and allowing—even encouraging—people to be themselves. It means investing in your employees to coach and help grow their skills. These initiatives create the difference in an organization's culture, and determine what the organization will become.

The SHC's approach to managing and resolving conflict, as with everything else they did, was passed from the staff to the guests, as you will see. Staff listened to customers the way their leaders listened to them. They welcomed feedback and had no problem doing whatever was necessary to turn a situation around. On top of that, the way the SHC managed staff conflict saved the organization from a lot of drama that often comes up in business. There were few silos or cliques within the organization, and there was no rumor mill. Staff were generally open with each other and with their bosses, and that made for healthy, productive relationships based on communication, trust, and respect.

The most important lesson from the SHC on managing difficult people and conflicts is simple: Don't ignore it. When conflicts are ignored, the result is always the same, whether it happens in a business, a marriage, or any relationship: The problems get worse. Dale and Stuart didn't avoid tough situations or people. They knew these things were part of the equation in business, and they dealt with them head-on. Of course, there were times when problems couldn't be resolved and mavericks weren't worth the effort. When that happened, they cut their losses, but never without first making the effort to find a resolution.

To better manage difficult people and constructively resolve staff conflicts in your organization, try the following:

1. *Jump in the ring.* Let your people know that you want to know when there is a conflict. They should feel that they are invited to come to you when there is an issue. Listen to them and resist the urge to dismiss what they are telling you, even if you think they are wrong. Instead, make a plan for resolution. That may mean more investigation; or it may require a mediation or curative coaching. Whatever the case, take the issues seriously and let your staff know that you do.

2. *Manage your mavericks.* If there is one person in your organization that you want to monitor closely, it's your high-performing maverick. Mavericks are valuable, even essential to an organization's growth, but they can come at a high price if leaders aren't prepared to be flexible and to actively manage the conflicts that inevitably arise. When you have a valuable maverick on board, make sure there are parameters around

what they are allowed to do, even if those parameters don't apply to anyone else. That may mean creating unique systems in which they operate, or having them coached on a weekly basis. The key is to allow them to bring their creative ideas to the table without creating chaos.

3. *Create agreements and check-ins for curative coaching and mediation.* Just having a talk with staff members who are problematic or not getting along does next to nothing. People may change for a day or so, but then they are back to old behaviors. Behavioral change requires specific commitments and a mechanism for holding people accountable to those commitments. Take Weight Watchers, for example. It works for millions of people because they have a specific goal and a plan for getting there, and they have to come to meetings every week and weigh in. The same is true for any other behavior. When coaching or mediating there should be between three to ten concrete agreements. These agreements should be monitored on a weekly basis for at least four to twelve weeks to ensure they stick. Make sure your managers or HR personnel are trained in effective mediation techniques. If necessary, consider bringing in outside professionals to mediate difficult conflicts and coach your staff.

PRINCIPLE 5:
CREATE A CULTURE OF CARE

IF YOU THINK ABOUT WHAT MATTERS MOST in your life, it's probably three things: health, relationships, and finances.

Now think about how many hours of your life you spend working. If you're like most people, work supports your finances, and your job consumes the largest share of your days—if you take sleep out of the equation, the average person spends more time at work than with the people they love. This takes a toll on relationships. Work can also take a toll on our health, either because of the nature of the work or simply because we are unhappy in our job. As important as work is, it's fair to say that, for many people, it creates a conflict between life's priorities, with our health and relationships paying the price for our need to earn a living.

This conflict can feel intractable. But what if a business took into account all three priorities? What if coming to work involved financial growth, helped create healthy relationships inside and outside of work, and supported physical health? Wouldn't that, in turn, make us work harder, do better, and give more?

The answer is yes.

The leaders of the SHC knew this intuitively. They didn't sit around in a room and concoct formulas to coerce their staff to provide better customer service and be more productive. They just cared about their people, simply and honestly, and used that as the basis for how they treated people. I don't think it ever occurred to them to do otherwise.

Since working with the SHC, I give the same simple piece of advice in all my seminars on leadership: *Care for your people exactly the way you want them to care for your customers.*

This care for others is the emotional core of Emotional Equity. Not only did it build a tremendous sense of loyalty to the organization, it became the foundation of the way the staff interacted with the SHC's guests, so that both the organization and the guest experience were defined by a culture of care. This culture was so powerful, the SHC would often receive heartfelt and moving letters from the guests about how much the staff had impacted them.

When I interviewed guests for this book, I heard many amazing stories. One in particular I will never forget: Deb Keble and her husband had booked a stay at the SHC for what was to be their first visit to Key West. But a few months before the trip, their son, a volunteer firefighter, had been killed in an accident. Though still in the throes of grief, Deb and her husband kept their reservation at the advice of friends and made the trip down to Key West from Pennsylvania. Not long after they arrived, Deb went to read by one of the pools. While she was there, a pool server named Heather noticed that Deb was using the prayer card from her son's funeral as a bookmark. Instead of shying away or pretending she didn't see it, Heather asked Deb if she was okay. Deb answered honestly: No, she was not okay.

Heather sat with Deb beside the pool and listened to Deb's story—not from a hospitality perspective, but from deep human care.

"Heather and everyone else at the hotel respected what we were going through," Deb told me. "They put their arms around us. It was the healing that we needed so much at that moment. We certainly were not expecting it, but I can assure you, I will always remember it."

The SHC's culture of care cascaded from Executive Committee down to the frontline staff. It was inherent in the leaders' philosophy that nothing mattered more than their people, and that it is impossible to make an arbitrary distinction between work life and personal life. They genuinely cared about the well-being of their people, and they saw it as their goal to nurture them and to help them grow.

While Dale and Stuart did many things over the years to create their culture of care, four practices stand out: They built relationships with their staff; they supported their people in times of need; they helped their people grow financially; and they contributed to their physical and mental health. Together, these practices and the culture they fostered made the SHC a place where life's priorities were no longer in conflict.

BUILD RELATIONSHIPS WITH YOUR STAFF

In their famous book *The Carrot Principle*, Adrian Gostick and Chester Elton highlight dozens of studies that demonstrate how promoting personal connection within an organization positively impacts business success. They write, "While managers fear that making an emotional connection with people will show weakness, nothing could be further from the truth. Today, the more we manage on the emotional side of the ledger, the more effective our leadership style is."

This directly contradicts the conventional wisdom still taught in most business schools. I remember sitting in a lecture hall at Columbia University as one of the renowned professors in my Master's program warned us against blurring the lines between personal and professional lives. It was a recipe for disaster in business, he assured us. He was preaching to the converted. My classmates and I nodded in agreement. We had all heard this before, and it seemed to make perfect sense. The idea that getting too involved with your staff personally could create the perception of favoritism and lead to silos made sense to me. I took that advice to heart, and for many years after that I often talked to my coaching clients about the need to keep work separate from personal issues.

All of that was turned upside down when I met the Executive Committee at the SHC. They established strong emotional connections with many of their staff, and they often got involved with what was going on in employees' lives outside of work. If someone was struggling, the leaders of the SHC wanted to know about it, instead of lecturing people to leave their personal problems at home.

When Stuart found out that longtime staff members who were a married couple had split up, he sought each of them out personally to see what they needed. Dale often asked people about their lives, children, and hobbies. Matt, Carrie and Adelheid visited staff members when they were sick, and they regularly invited people into their offices to talk when they had something going on in their personal lives. Staff felt that their leaders honestly cared about them as people, and they showed the same care to each other and to guests in turn. I remember a staff member moving into a new apartment on her own for the first time after a long marriage had painfully ended. Her colleagues showed up without prompting to help her move furniture, decorate and settle in. That kind of act was typical at the SHC.

Of course, too much personal connection could be inappropriate, and that's where I saw the leaders draw the line of professionalism. The care they showed to their employees was personal, but it never turned into a friendship. "I have always had a personal relationship with the people who work for me," says Dale. "But I never made them my regular, social friends. And I don't think you should. Instead, I became paternal to them and mentored them. They were valued business colleagues, not close, intimate personal friends."

That distinction finally helped me understand this principle of Emotional Equity. Making genuine personal connections in your business isn't about being pals with your subordinates. Rather, it's about mentoring people and helping them to grow, both at work and in their lives outside of work.

Once I understood it, this approach made more sense than the conventional wisdom I had accepted at the start of my career. I had discovered what the leaders of the SHC already knew: People can't be split into separate personal and professional entities, because the two spheres of life are completely intertwined. To really engage your employees and help them grow, you need to mentor them both professionally and personally. This is the foundation of effective leadership, as Gostick and Elton noted, and the first step in building your culture of care.

HELP YOUR PEOPLE IN TIMES OF NEED
(AND DON'T WAIT UNTIL THEY ASK)

There are two types of giving: the one born from a request, and the other from observation.

Most leaders wait until they are asked to offer help to their employees. Maybe that's because they don't want to intrude, or they are afraid of starting down a slippery slope. Or maybe they have so much on their own plates that they don't see when people need assistance, whether on the job or outside of work. Whatever the case, it's a missed opportunity.

When leaders offer help before people ask for it, the practice creates trust, loyalty, dedication, and a sense of shared purpose that is difficult to describe. This was evident at the SHC, where the Executive Committee was always ready to help an employee in need. Even with a staff of 250, the leaders of the SHC often knew when someone was struggling in their lives. They understood how hard it could be to ask for help, so they never hesitated to get involved.

In my first few months working with the Executive Committee, one of their key people suffered a nervous breakdown. It started with missed workdays, followed by emotional outbursts, erratic behavior, and finally a suicide attempt. Carrie was the woman's direct boss. She rushed to the hospital, called her daily, went to her house, and arranged for therapy—even after the employee told her she probably would not come back to work. This kind of outreach was not a one-time event. The Executive Committee often got involved when there was a serious problem with a valued staff member. They lent people money, counseled them, checked in on them—and on occasion, even bailed them out of jail.

For many years I have worked with another group of hotels in Key West called Historic Key West Inns. Their operations manager, Marlon Garnett, takes the same approach. When his employees are in need, he is the first one to show up. He does it quietly, but he makes sure his people know they are supported. Once in a while, a staff member will confide in me that Marlon gave him money when he was down and out; or Marlon showed up at the hospital when someone wasn't well; or he gave money to someone's church. These acts of kindness make the staff fiercely loyal to the company and inspire them to treat each other and the guests in the same way.

I witnessed countless examples of this in the years I worked with the SHC. One that stands out is the case of a young manager, Julie.

A few years after Dale and Stuart bought the Southernmost Beach Café, they recognized the need to provide health insurance for their staff. Few, if any, stand-alone restaurants in Key West offered health insurance, so there was no market pressure to provide it, but they wanted their employees to have that security. The challenge was finding an affordable plan. While they were researching their options, something happened to create urgency: Julie, one of their key managers, got pregnant and was in a difficult situation with very little support.

When Dale found out, he asked her for a meeting. "He told me, 'You're not alone,'" recalls Julie. "He assured me that he and Stuart were going to figure something out . . . I was completely shocked that he reached out to me in this way. It made me feel so supported during a really rough time in my life."

Two months later, the Café had a new health insurance plan that covered 90 percent of maternity and cost employees only $18 per month. "I could not believe what they had done," says Julie. "This encapsulates how they think. Instead of just making a difference in my life, they saw an opportunity to make a difference in the whole company."

Julie's story is typical of the Executive Committee's proactive approach to offering help to employees. On a few occasions they helped staff members deal with substance abuse and addiction problems, which are not uncommon in a party town like Key West. When these issues came to the leaders' attention, they stepped in right away and offered to pay for counseling or help with treatment costs for rehabilitation. They knew the intervention might not work, or that the employee might leave the organization; but, when they believed the person could beat his/her addiction, they did whatever they could to help.

The SHC's leaders' attention to their employees' needs and willingness to offer help came through in everyday situations, too.

"One day it was absolutely pouring rain at the end of my shift," recalls Dexter Womble, former Front Desk agent. "Stuart was going somewhere and stopped in. We chatted about the rain and he asked me if I had a rain coat. He knew I wasn't driving. When he found out I didn't have a jacket, he insisted that I take his. I refused, and he finally told me to go his room and take any jacket I wanted in the closet. I will never forget that."

That kind of astute observation and care cascaded down through the entire organization.

"Matt lived and breathed the staff. He was great with us. He knew us, and went to bat for us even when we didn't ask him to," says Lena Warner, former Controller. "Carrie did the same. She actually doted on her staff. In turn, they doted on the guests and cared for each other."

The guests at the SHC often commented on the level of genuine care they received from the staff. The front lines took great pride in anticipating guests' needs, and often reveled in staff meetings about a moment in which they could do something that surprised and delighted a guest.

One morning, an elderly French couple was sitting in the lobby, trying to fix a problem on their laptop computer. The couple had come to the SHC to celebrate their 50th wedding anniversary. It was the trip of a lifetime for them, but they were clearly in distress as they struggled with the laptop. The staff noticed and checked in to see if they needed help. The couple explained that they wanted to send their children and grandchildren photos of their trip, but something had gone wrong with their computer. They were heartbroken by the thought that they couldn't reach out to their families to share this important occasion with them.

Adelheid and Duane Webster, the IT manager, heard what was happening and got involved. Duane asked if they would mind leaving the computer with him for a few hours. Then Adelheid escorted the couple to the garden of the Dewey House and treated them to an anniversary breakfast, before sending them off to the beach for the afternoon, including a special lunch on the hotel. In the meantime, Duane set to work on the laptop, determined to get it fixed even if he had to take it apart piece by piece. Later that afternoon, he and Adelheid returned the laptop to the couple—completely fixed and tuned so it functioned even better. Duane still remembers the couple's surprise and joy when he handed the computer back to them in perfect working order.

"I'm sure we lost money, spending all that time and effort," says Duane. "But we did it because we wanted them to have the time of their lives with us. The look on their faces when we fixed it made it all worth it."

Offering help before people ask is a sure way to elevate any relationship to new heights. It means that the person giving is really in tune with the person being helped. It takes the awkwardness of asking for something out of the equation. It is an evolved way of giving with its roots steeped in something deeper and more meaningful than money: It is an expression of a fundamental belief in doing the right thing because it is right.

The more the Executive Committee at the SHC practiced this form of giving with their staff, the more their staff practiced it with the SHC's guests—and the stronger the SHC's culture of care evolved.

HELP YOUR PEOPLE GROW FINANCIALLY

It is common knowledge that money is not the number one motivator for employees. Studies show that an increase in salary leads to a morale boost in the workplace of no more than two months. Still, money matters, and people won't work well, happily, or long without fair compensation.

Dale and Stuart believed in helping their people to grow in many ways, and that included their finances. They realized that if they wanted a long-term commitment from their staff, they needed to help them in any way possible.

Many big corporations offer 401(k) plans and shares of their company as part of their compensation packages, but small organizations rarely have that luxury. Dale and Stuart found a way around this limitation by doing three things: They rewarded key people with equity in the business, offered longtime members of their management team an opportunity to invest in the business, and gave their staff at all levels of the organization unexpected bonuses. Over time, these efforts helped many staff members secure their financial futures.

It started with Matt and Carrie. By the end of the first decade of their tenure at the SHC, the couple had two children, a home on the waterfront, and a great reputation in the community. Life in Key West was good, but they didn't necessarily see themselves staying there forever. Dale and Stuart knew this. They also understood the value of Matt and Carrie, so they devised a way to incentivize Matt and Carrie to make the SHC their career.

"I told them we wanted to keep them and give them stake in the organization," says Dale. "We gave them each 2 percent equity," recalls Dale. "It changed their minds about leaving. I knew it would create dedication, loyalty, and security. It is good business to invest in the people that make up your company."

For Matt and Carrie, the equity offer changed the way they thought about their roles at the SHC. They no longer just worked there; now they were part of it.

"I felt like I owned the hotel," says Matt. "That made a big difference."

Offering equity to the General Managers of a hotel isn't unprecedented in the industry. More unusual was the fact that Dale and Stuart gave other employees at the SHC an opportunity to invest with them in another business. This happened in 2007, when they decided to purchase the restaurant that would become the Southernmost Beach Café. Their equity partners in the SHC didn't want to be involved in the restaurant business, so Dale and Stuart considered other ways to put together the $375,000 they needed to close the deal. They had many options for raising the capital, but after considering the traditional routes, they decided to offer shares to a few long-term members of the SHC's management team.

"We gave up 40 percent of the restaurant," explains Stuart. "It seemed like a good idea to give that opportunity to our own people. We were counting on the fact that, virtually, it would be a very profitable investment for them."

It was a risky move that could have led to problems if the restaurant had failed, but the veterans of the SHC's management team had faith that Dale and Stuart could transform the Café, just like they had done for the SHC itself.

That faith proved to be well founded. When the Café sold in 2013, some of the staff that had invested just six years earlier received life-changing returns on their investments.

"In our wildest dreams, we didn't think we would run the revenue up as high as we did," says Stuart. "It made me very happy to see our people get that money."

There were other financial situations in which Dale and Stuart went beyond even their usual above-and-beyond approach to support their people.

Soon after the purchase of the Café, Adelheid and her family decided to move to Ecuador. As an important member of the SHC's management team, Adelheid was one of the investors in the Café. She decided to sell her shares in the Café back to Dale and Stuart before leaving.

Things in Ecuador didn't work out the way Adelheid and her family had planned. Nor did they work out with her replacement at the SHC. Dale suggested that Matt contact Adelheid to discuss the possibility of coming back to the SHC. Adelheid said she was interested, but the expense of getting resettled in Key West was too high. When Dale and Stuart found out, they offered to pay the family's moving expenses. Soon after that, and much to the delight of everyone at the SHC, Adelheid returned. Dale and Stuart not only helped her get on her feet again, they loaned her the money to repurchase her shares in the Café.

"Adelheid was critical to our success, and we wanted her to have every opportunity to thrive," says Dale. "At that point, we didn't need to give her back the shares, but we wanted her to have them."

Adelheid remained in her position until 2013, when the hotel sold. "I hadn't planned on this career," she admits, "but they created a culture that made people want to stay."

For the rest of the staff, Dale and Stuart used a generous discretionary bonus system that gave them and the management team the flexibility to reward people for a job well done, and as a way to share the hotel's success with the people who worked hard on the front lines to make it happen. "If we prospered, the staff prospered," says Dale. This practice culminated in the more than $1 million Dale and Stuart gave to the staff after selling the SHC to LaSalle. The bankers who cut the "thank you" checks said they had never seen anything like it.

Not long after giving out the bonus checks, Todd Jones, the SHC's Front Desk Manager, called Dale and Stuart to thank them for their generosity. Todd had lived in Key West more than two decades, but had always rented. The bonus from the sale had helped him and his partner buy a house.

"It made me feel so good to know that," says Stuart. "I felt like we really made a difference."

Making a difference was the purpose of the discretionary bonus program, and of all Dale and Stuart's efforts to help their staff grow financially. They understood that their people could go work for corporate-owned hotels and restaurants on the island, places that could offer 401(k) programs and employee stock options and other perks that the SHC couldn't match. What they could do, however, was be creative and flexible in ways that their larger competitors couldn't. This flexibility enabled them to incentivize and reward their staff for loyalty and hard work in authentic and meaningful ways.

CONTRIBUTE TO YOUR EMPLOYEES' MENTAL AND PHYSICAL WELLNESS

Most organizations have some kind of wellness program in place. It's common practice now for employees to get complimentary

Fitbits, subsidized or discounted gym memberships, and even free exercise classes. Offering such programs is smart. According to the World Health Organization, business losses due to employee illnesses can reach up to $300 billion annually in the U.S. alone. Wellness programs have the potential to save businesses a lot of money and improve overall productivity.

On top of the savings that come from fewer employee sick days, an effective wellness program can significantly improve teamwork and staff morale in an organization. Studies on exercise show that team sports are among the most effective forms of physical activity for promoting wellness, and at the same time they raise morale, improve relationships, and encourage success. This makes sense. Think about how much more motivated you are to perform well when you have a group of people cheering you on, then compare that to the tedium of exercising alone.

The leaders of the SHC took this idea and ran with it.

When Dale and Stuart decided to create a wellness program, they first looked at hiring an outside contractor, but none of the providers they interviewed impressed them. Dale then asked Adelheid if she would develop something. She said yes, and took to the challenge with vigor. Like Dale and Stuart, she knew it would be a tremendous benefit for the staff, and for the organization as a whole.

Instead of taking a one-size-fits-all approach, Adelheid designed the SHC's wellness program based on the staff's needs. A group of staff members wanted to quit smoking, so the program sponsored a hypnosis series on smoking cessation. Other staff wanted to lose weight and be more fit, so the leaders brought in a consultant to do biometric screening, and Stuart bought everyone who was interested a copy of a weight-loss program that had worked for him.

And then there was the Ragnar Relay race. The Ragnar Relay is a worldwide race event that organizes 200-mile team races in every terrain imaginable, including a race that starts in Miami and ends in Key West. Under Adelheid's guidance, the hotel organized a twelve-person team and entered the race. The runners trained together for months, and the entire organization rallied behind them. On the day of the race, almost every hotel staff member came out to cheer on their team. The energy and support was fantastic, and the good vibe lasted for weeks thereafter.

In addition to the goodwill and camaraderie, the Ragnar incited a company-wide fitness movement. The team continued to train together after the race, and other staff members began to join the group. Stuart noticed right away. He came to me shortly after the race and said he wanted to sponsor more teams next year.

When the next Ragnar Relay rolled around, the SHC had thirty staff members running. The excitement and support for the team was unbelievable. The organization assumed the entire bill for the race, and even went one step further: Carrie surprised everyone by booking the team in rooms at the Ritz Carlton in Miami, and took everyone out for dinner the night before the event. She and Matt then drove hundreds of miles to meet the runners throughout the two grueling days and cheer them on.

"This wasn't just some wellness event you see organizations do all the time," says Duane Webster. "This was blood and sweat— and it was real. It put us into a healthier mindset, and it made a difference because it wasn't imposed on us. It came from us."

Beyond the Ragnar Relay, the SHC sponsored its staff in any athletic events people chose to participate in. Employees began running 5Ks, marathons, and triathlons. Those who couldn't run began walking. People throughout the organization began eating more healthy food and losing weight. The fitness movement was irresistibly positive and supportive. The biggest number of participants in fitness classes came from the women in Housekeeping. As a whole, the staff had never been healthier.

Over time, the wellness program became one of the cornerstones of its culture of care. In retrospect, Adelheid describes these efforts as the "best management decision we ever made."

HOW TO CREATE A CULTURE OF CARE IN YOUR ORGANIZATION

First and foremost, a culture of care has to be genuine. If your goal is solely to produce a better, more motivated workforce, you are missing the point. *You* have to care, or the culture and its benefits will never come to fruition.

Second, you need to let go of the old-school thinking that says you should not get involved with your employees. This doesn't mean you should hang out with your staff on the weekend or party with them after work; you still have to maintain appropriate boundaries. But those boundaries should never create impersonal relationships. You need to know how many kids your employees have, what they love to do when they are not working, what they aspire to, and what inspires them.

Here are a few simple and inexpensive practices from the SHC that can help you to cultivate a culture of care:

1. ***Do regular pulse checks with your staff.*** Walk around every couple of days and just spend a few minutes here and there, learning more about your staff. Find out what they like to do, what they love, what their lives outside of work are like. There's no need to go deep into their private lives—you aren't there to fix their problems or be a shoulder to cry on—but you need to know what's going on with your people. It is possible

to maintain appropriate social boundaries and form genuine personal relationships; this should be your goal. Be a mentor and a resource for help when they need it.

2. *Look for opportunities to offer help.* If you see a need, try to offer assistance. If you know a staff member is moving houses, you might offer to send a mover, or gather a team of colleagues to help. If a team member is expecting a baby, find out what she needs and throw her a baby shower. If it's raining and a person doesn't have an umbrella, offer them yours. Providing help before people ask for it builds and strengthens relationships. Your example will inspire your staff to do the same for others.

3. *Seek ways to help your people grow financially and improve their health.* Relationships, health, and finances are the three most important priorities in life. Part of creating a culture of care is doing what you reasonably can to take all of them into account. It isn't always possible to offer equity shares or institute a discretionary bonus program, but if you keep an open mind you might find other opportunities to reward your staff in unexpected ways. And don't underestimate the positive impact a wellness program can have on employee health, teamwork, and morale. Again, you might not be able to fund an expensive investment in this area; but if you ask your people what activities they are interested in and tailor your efforts specifically to those things, you will likely find that there are many simple, inexpensive things you can do to support their health and wellness.

.

PRINCIPLE 6:
RADICAL HOSPITALITY

IT'S ONE THING TO PROVIDE GREAT CUSTOMER SERVICE; it's something else entirely to imbue your staff with the genuine desire to go above and beyond for your customers. The former is based on standards and protocols; the latter comes from deeply held values, inspiration, and a sense of purpose.

At the SHC, service defined the spirit of the organization. The SHC hit the top of social media sites not because of their property and amenities, but because the resort and its staff provided an experience that gave people, as their motto read, "the time of their lives." One longtime guest, Lena Haar, who traveled around the world staying in fine hotels, termed this experience "radical hospitality."

Radical hospitality was rooted in the SHC's culture of care. Staff connected personally with guests, they paid attention to what guests wanted and needed, and they went out of their way to meet those needs. Because of the Executive Committee's willingness to empower their people, employees at all levels had the freedom to be creative in making sure guests felt at home and truly did have the time of their lives during their stay. This personalized care and attention is what set the SHC apart from its competition and created that special feeling that made the experience meaningful for staff and guests alike. It was not uncommon to see guests give staff members a hug before departing for the airport. Many of the survey responses the hotel received about the staff sounded more like love letters than customer reviews.

On one occasion, a guest visited Key West after nursing her father in his battle with terminal cancer. No one knew this during her stay; but as was typical, when the staff saw how tired she was, they took excellent care of her and showed an authentic interest in making sure she got well-needed rest. Upon her return home, she wrote a letter explaining her situation and thanking the staff for reminding her of "all the good there is in the world."

When I read these words to the frontline staff in one of their monthly meetings, half the room welled up with tears. This wasn't something one sees typically in a hotel, or in any business, but the SHC received these kinds of sentiments from guests on a regular basis.

"I love my job because I actually get to make a difference," says Cindy Spencer, Front Desk agent. "People who come to Key West are often celebrating life's biggest occasions or trying to recover from a tough time. We get newlyweds and veterans all in the same day. Remembering that about our guests helps me. It makes what I do feel important."

The goal of SHC was to tap in to a deeper sense of what brings meaning to peoples' lives, and to use that to make every day matter. Sometimes that meant doing something as simple as buying an ice cream cone from the shop across the street when a guest mentioned that he wanted to try one. Other times, it meant building relationships with customers over a long period of time and getting to know their families.

"I have never seen a hotel that takes such good care of its people," says longtime patron Stephen Lane. "They go out of their way to know the guests and to cater to individual needs. And it's not put on. It's the real deal."

How did the SHC accomplish what all businesses aspire to do with their customer service? It wasn't luck. Radical hospitality and the customer satisfaction and loyalty it created were the hard-earned results of consistent effort and unwavering commitment.

The SHC's culture of radical hospitality was based on five key things: The first was creating a formal, ongoing program to focus on customer service; the second was making the customer service program matter to people's lives; the third was letting the staff be creative in serving customers; the fourth was becoming a "community sweetheart" in Key West; and the fifth was having 100 percent backing from leadership. Together, these five practices provide a template you can use to create your own culture of radical hospitality.

CREATE A CUSTOMER SERVICE PROGRAM (NOT JUST TRAINING)

For the first ten years of my career, I called myself a trainer, not a consultant. I traveled around the world teaching workshops for businesses ranging from Fortune 500 Companies to multi-national humanitarian organizations. People were often on an emotional high when we finished, and they left the workshops ready to make positive changes in their organizations. But the euphoria and motivation were short-lived: When I checked back in six months or a year, most of what I had taught wasn't being practiced. I soon learned that one workshop or training session rarely leads to a permanent change. It's like anything in life: Lasting change requires consistent and continuous effort—no one ever lost weight by dieting for a day. I wanted to do more than provide one-time workshops and training; I wanted to have an opportunity to create lasting change, and to see the results.

That opportunity arrived when Dale and Stuart hired me to help improve customer service at the SHC. Dale told me point-blank that he wanted an ongoing program, not a one-shot deal; he knew that one-time training was a waste of time and money. My original engagement with the hotel was for six months, during which time I would provide training and put in place ongoing systems to reinforce the lessons of the training and ensure that the new practices became permanent.

This was music to my ears. Finally, here was someone in a leadership role who was interested in the principles I was teaching *and* willing to pay me to make sure it all stuck.

There was one problem: No one had ever asked me to do this before, so I would have to make it up as I went along. Fortunately, Dale and Stuart supported the process 100 percent.

The program, which we called Exceptional Customer Service, or ECS, grew organically, with a lot of input and guidance from the Executive Committee. In the end, we identified eight key components that became the foundation of the SHC's radical hospitality:

1. *A standard 2.5-hour training session.* The point of this training session was to introduce the foundational concepts of the ECS program—the twenty points of service every staff member was expected to practice at all times, and the "Life Happiness Approach" to Customer Service—and to

get everyone speaking the same language about customer service. The training was high energy and interactive, and meaningful. (More about that last point when we talk about the "Life Happiness Approach" in detail.)

Most people arrived for the training with a look on their face that said they would rather be anywhere else, only to leave full of energy and enthusiasm. The training material itself provided tools and tips the staff could refer back to later, as they worked to put the ECS principles into practice. Furthermore, the concepts didn't just apply to work; ECS gave people a set of tools they could use in every relationship in their lives. The ECS training made everyone part of a community with shared values that were explicitly stated and discussed, and it required them to be their best selves.

2. ***ECS Departmental Goals.*** Each department at the SHC had a numerical goal that was used to measure how well the department was serving customers. Guests would fill out surveys and rate the various aspects of their stay at the hotel. Scores for each department were averaged monthly, and the results were compared against the department's goal. This approach helped to make an inherently qualitative experience like customer service quantifiable. It gave people a solid number to work toward, and helped the departments rally around a common goal.

Having a target proved to be a powerful motivator; it gave people direction and purpose and destination to aim for. (As Yogi Berra said, "If you don't know where you're going, you probably won't get there.") At the beginning of the month, staff would stop me on property to ask if I had received the ECS scores yet—the goals and the scores were that meaningful to them.

If a department met its goals three months in a row, everyone in the department was given a small reward from the hotel to thank them for their efforts. Stuart used to tell them, "We're not giving you a reward as a carrot. You set your own goal and we expect you to work towards it. The ECS rewards are just a way of letting you know how much we appreciate what you do."

Early in the process we announced that the housekeeping staff had met their goals three months in a row. The housekeeping staff literally jumped out of their chairs and hooted and hollered. I think even Matt was taken aback by the reaction. It was a critical moment for me, when I realized that the staff had really bought in. They cared deeply about meeting their goals.

3. *Monthly ECS Review at Staff Meetings.* Every department met on a monthly basis. The agenda for these monthly department meetings always included logistics and updates from the managers and an in-depth review of all things ECS-related. In addition to reviewing the department's ECS scores from the previous month, TripAdvisor reviews, internal survey results, and other details, I would teach a brief lesson on a new ECS skill or topic, to ensure that we were always growing the staff's skill set. I covered everything from "Managing Stress" to "Understanding Personality Types" to "'Building Rapport." The meetings were interactive and fun. The managers always asked the staff for their ideas on how to make things better for them and the guests. I knew staff wanted and needed those questions, and often they talked about how much they appreciated being asked for their input.

The meetings were an opportunity to recognize staff who had been mentioned in positive reviews and surveys.

Matt had chocolate bars made with custom SHC wrappers. He would read aloud the great reviews in which people were mentioned by name, then personally hand out the chocolate to those staff members and shake their hands. I thought this was simply a nice touch until one day one of the Front Desk agents said to me, "Everyone is always hoping for a chocolate bar—not because we care about the candy, but because it feels like we're getting a block of gold." The personal recognition and thanks turned a simple candy bar into something almost priceless.

4. ***ECS Cards.*** Each staff member was given a pocket-size card with the twenty points of service printed on it. Staff were required to carry their card and know the twenty points. Management spot-checked to make sure everyone had their cards and referred to them often.

5. ***Manager Observation Checklists.*** Managers in each department created a checklist of skills and tools that their staff needed to know to provide great service. If individuals or a department was struggling, the observation checklists were used as part of the remediation process (see Principle 3: Accountability). Managers would periodically observe their staff and use the checklist to assess their performance, then share the feedback with them. For example, if the Front Desk had received a series of tough reviews on TripAdvisor, or if the department's ECS scores dipped, the manager or I would do observations for everyone in the department over a period of two or three weeks to tighten things up and get the staff back on track.

6. ***Secret Shoppers.*** The Café was secret-shopped on a monthly basis, and the hotel was shopped quarterly. The information from the reports was shared at ECS meetings to help improve

service. More importantly, the Executive Committee made it a priority to immediately share the results of a secret shop with the staff members who had been shopped and their managers, and they used the ideas and feedback from the experience to make changes right away. The secret shoppers helped us drill down to a level of detail that other feedback channels couldn't address. As a result, we were able to really fine-tune the operation.

The Executive Committee also used this feedback for training purposes. At every ECS meeting, the managers or I read the surveys to the whole team and talked about what we did well and what we could be doing better.

7. *Management and Leadership Training.* The Executive Committee expected every manager at the SHC to treat their people as well as they expected their people to treat the guests. Some managers were naturals at this, but most needed to learn how to do this. Early in the process, Dale and Stuart suggested that I do regular training sessions for the managers on motivating employees, communication, conflict resolution, mediation, stress management, and other leadership topics. These training sessions were held quarterly. They helped the managers buy in to the ECS process and reinforce it with their staff, and they also helped the managers become more active in creating the SHC's underlying culture of care.

8. *Active Follow-Up on Guest Surveys and Social Media.* Once the ECS process was up and running, there were few days when I didn't hear from Dale or Stuart about a comment or issue from the guest surveys. They read the surveys almost as fast as they came in. If we got a great survey about a staff member, it was shared with them immediately. Conversely,

there was a system in place for addressing every significant negative comment from a guest. The Guest Relations Manager was responsible for making sure department managers shared that information with their people, and then followed up with her directly to confirm that the survey feedback was delivered. This system of "no review unturned" made it clear to everyone in the organization that leadership was actively engaged in the ECS process and always knew what was going on.

The eight components described above are what I now give in a handbook to leaders when I begin my work with them. I have used these components to replicate the ECS program in numerous hotels and restaurants, as well as businesses outside the hospitality industry. In all cases, these businesses have improved their customer satisfaction and retention rates, and their bottom lines.

Nothing in the ECS program should come as a surprise to you. The key to its success is not novelty, but consistent practice. Radical hospitality, like everything else in Emotional Equity, is ultimately about creating culture by changing patterns of behavior. These changes don't happen overnight or in one-off training sessions; it takes dedication and commitment day after day to make them stick.

MAKE CUSTOMER SERVICE MATTER TO PEOPLE'S LIVES

No one gets excited about coming to a customer service seminar. The frontline staff in any business are working hard every day dealing with people who aren't always easy to serve, and they're not getting rich doing it. The last thing these staff members need is a preachy classroom lecture on how to smile and be nice.

Not surprisingly, when I started the ECS training at the SHC, I wasn't the most popular kid in school.

"At first, I hated the sight of Elisa Levy," admits Duane Webster. Duane certainly wasn't alone. I knew the majority of the staff would be either indifferent or resistant to ECS training at first. This didn't bother me. My job is 70 percent motivation, 30 percent teaching. I knew the staff would only learn the ECS skills through repetition, and they wouldn't put in the effort to consistently repeat the skills if they didn't want them in the first place. It was up to me to convince everyone that they wanted these skills.

This isn't as hard as it might seem. The trick is to understand what motivates people. The simplest answer is probably what Freud said: Human beings seek pleasure and avoid pain. We all want to be happy, especially in our relationships with other people. Customer service skills are really relationships skills— communication, resolving conflict, making a personal connection, and being positive. To make people care about customer service skills, I simply had to reframe them in a different context, one that connected with their innate desire to be happy.

I started with a question: "Does anyone want to be happier in life? In your relationships? At work?"

Everyone in the room raised a hand, even the people sitting with arms crossed.

"Well," I said, "this is the stuff that makes your life better." Then everyone listened more closely.

"ECS taught us values," says Todd Jones. "I compare it to what I learn in church in terms of how to do good in the world and treat people. It was about life lessons that made us treat each other and guests with genuine care and respect."

The seminar, which I now call "The Life Happiness Approach to Customer Service," is interactive, engaging, and fun. I use examples from customers, of course, and also from marriages, parenting, and mother-in-law situations. It doesn't always win over everyone, but it usually hits home for the majority.

"Most of us really did not want to go to a training session, but when we realized that we could apply the skills to our personal lives, we wanted to learn," says former SHC Guest Relations Manager Colleen Mulligan. "I use the tools at work and in my life, and I have taught them to my family members."

Colleen's experience isn't unusual. In the years since I started using the "Life Happiness Approach" for ECS training, many of the staff members at the SHC and other organizations where I've given the seminar have reached out to let me know they have used the concepts and tools to transform relationships and themselves.

I've seen the ECS program work in different businesses across different industries. At the SHC the approach was especially effective, because it was in line with what the leaders genuinely wanted for their people.

"It was genius to incorporate our personal lives into our ECS program," says Sam Messier, former innkeeper for La Mer and Dewey House. "It allowed me to understand myself better and how to live well. It was about basic rules on how to treat people, and it changed my relationships at home and work."

The Life Happiness Approach even won over Duane Webster, who initially hated the sight of me. About six years later, when Duane was running his own successful business, I received a text from him out of the blue, telling me how often he used the skills he learned in ECS in his new business and with his family. It was yet another reminder of the core of Emotional Equity: If you focus on building genuine relationships and growing your people, good things will follow.

Other business owners know this, too. In his famous book, *Setting the Table*, restaurateur Danny Myers, who owns Gramercy Tavern and the Union Square Café in New York City, says that he always teaches his people that taking care of themselves and each other is "a higher priority than taking care of the guest." On the surface, it sounds like bad advice for a business; but if you understand the power of Emotional Equity, you will recognize that Myers' advice is actually the formula for success.

LET YOUR STAFF BE CREATIVE WITH CUSTOMER SERVICE

Not long ago I was having coffee with a friend who had listened to me *kvell* (Yiddish for brag) about the SHC for years. I was telling her a story about how a guest at the hotel had asked where he could buy the *New York Times*. The next morning, one of the pool attendants had arranged to have a copy of the newspaper waiting for the guest on his pool chair. When the guest saw it, he acted like someone had bought him a new car.

My friend said, "It's kind of like everyone there gets a fairy-tale magic wand they can use to make someone's day at will."

My friend had hit the nail on the head, only it wasn't a fairy tale—the magic was real. It came from the fact that the SHC's leaders empowered their people to be creative when it came to serving guests and solving problems. As a result, staff members went out of their way to perform random acts of kindness for guests, and for each other. Whatever form these random acts of kindness took, the goal was always the same: to surprise and delight.

Buying newspapers for guests at the pool was only one example. When a Front Desk agent learned that the father of a family checking in had just returned from serving in the war in Iraq and this was the first trip he was taking with his wife and children since his return, she personally wrote him a card expressing how much she appreciated what he had done for the country. The manager sent the family flowers.

When Sam Messier, the innkeeper for the SHC's bed-and-breakfast guesthouse, found out that a guest preferred almond milk, she stopped at the market the morning he was arriving and got some.

At the Southernmost Beach Café, the bartenders got together on their own to form an unofficial Fun Committee. The committee's task was to come up with one zany idea each week to help guests have a great time. One of their biggest hits was a pop quiz on Key West, with a free drink awarded to the winner.

None of these examples or the countless other random acts of kindness was institutionalized or prescribed. Like so much of how Emotional Equity was practiced at the SHC, they emerged organically and became part of the culture. The Executive Committee's constant focus on building relationships, empowerment, and caring for people translated directly into the staff's desire to surprise and delight the hotel's guests. And if staff members had an idea they weren't sure about, they simply went to their manager for guidance and approval. Most of the time, the answer was yes.

As with the culture of care, the SHC's commitment to radical hospitality started at the top. Dale and Stuart and the rest of the Executive Committee not only supported the staff's radical acts of kindness, they led by example. Often I would see the owners taking guests to dinner at the Café—not just treating them to a meal, but having it with them.

More importantly, the Executive Committee went out of its way to bring the same sense of surprise and delight to their own people. They helped host weddings, generously donated to the causes their staff members were involved in, and even went above and beyond for people who were relative newcomers new to the team, as I discovered when I was pregnant with my daughter. At that point, I had been working with the SHC as a consultant for about a year and a half. One day I showed up for a meeting with Matt and Carrie and they invited me to the conference room. Half the staff were there, the room was decorated with banners and balloons, there were chocolate cupcakes with chocolate icing (my favorite, as someone had secretly learned) and gifts wrapped in pastel pink. The scene was so unexpected that at first I didn't understand what was happening—the staff were throwing a baby shower . . . for me. Carrie had arranged it all.

I turned to her in amazement. I couldn't believe it. I was just a consultant, not a member of the staff. "Why did you do all this?" I asked.

"Because you are family," Carrie replied.

That was it, as cliché as it may sound. The magic of radical hospitality was that it made everyone who came to the SHC feel like family, special, and a person who mattered—because they did.

BE A COMMUNITY SWEETHEART

Radical hospitality is about more than serving customers and caring for your staff; it's also about the hospitality a business extends its community.

Many businesses miss this crucial element of community hospitality, especially when they cater to tourists. But like it or not, even in the day and age of social media, word-of-mouth recommendations from the people in your community carry more weight than just about anything. I'm aware of this every time I travel somewhere new. I always ask the locals what they think about the best places to stay and eat, and the best things to do. I make it a point to ask several different people. More often than not, I get the same responses—and more often than not, they're right.

In Key West, most businesses are community-minded, and they tend to take care of their local customers. They have locals-only discounts and specials, and some even offer priority seating and reservations to community members. All that helps with popularity, but only a few businesses can be the community's "sweethearts."

What is a community sweetheart? It's an organization that locals love because it is fundamental to the community itself; it is part of the culture. It's a business that partially defines what locals love about living there. Special seating and discounts alone don't make that happen. There needs to be a real relationship between the business and the community.

The SHC was one of Key West's favorite businesses among locals. There were a number of reasons. First, the resort was one of the biggest private contributors to local causes—no small feat in a town that is well known for philanthropy. They hosted fundraisers, concerts, celebrations, and participated in every island event possible. Community races started and ended at the Southernmost Beach Café. Dale and Stuart gave Matt and Carrie full authority to support any cause they wanted, and encouraged it.

"Our philosophy is that you ought to be good for the community, not just your business," says Stuart. "It benefited us, but that really wasn't the motive. It was general goodwill. We trusted that Matt and Carrie would give as they saw fit."

Second, Matt and Carrie were personally involved. Between them, they served on numerous boards of directors, from Hospice to the Lodging Association. In time, they became known as ambassadors of the Key West community.

The real clincher, and what made the business indispensable to the community, was that the SHC decided to champion their own cause and create a signature event. When Matt became the president of the Key West Rotary in 2009, he decided that they were going to organize the biggest fundraiser the Rotary had ever seen, with the proceeds going to fund local college scholarships and clean drinking water and polio-eradication projects in developing countries. The key to success would be to ascertain what would sell best in Key West. Matt knew the answer: beer. He led the Rotary in organizing Key West's first Brewfest. The event was held at the SHC, and vendors from all over the United States were invited to showcase their beers. The Rotary planned on a relatively small event that first year, and what they got was a surprise, even to them: The event sold out and netted $9,000. In following years, Brewfest grew bigger and began attracting tourists and raising more money with each year. By its third year, the event raised $58,000.

Locals looked forward to Brewfest every year and made plans to attend the event weeks, even months in advance. The community loved the fun of the event as much as they loved the cause it supported. It was a win-win for everyone.

How did all this help with radical hospitality? Just about any local you met in Key West would know all about the SHC. They would recommend it to strangers and friends, hold their weddings and parties at the hotel, and frequent the restaurant. The relationships the business built with the community were genuine, and they contributed to that special feeling that was shared by locals and tourists alike—the SHC was more than a hotel.

GET 100% SUPPORT FROM LEADERSHIP

The SHC was a great success story, but I've also experienced some failures. One of the biggest disappointments was a large company in the Keys whose owner had watched the SHC soar financially and on social media. He hired me to replicate for him, in his words, "exactly what you did for them." That sounded easy to me, so I jumped right in, riding high with the confidence that the ECS program and radical hospitality would work just like it had at the SHC. But to my surprise, it didn't happen. The frontline staff took issue with everything I asked of them, and the managers gave me even more resistance than their people.

I soon realized what the problem was: The owner didn't care about Emotional Equity, ECS, or radical hospitality; he just wanted the financial results. In his eyes, it was my job to come in and make things work. He had neither the inclination nor the desire to get involved and back the program, or even to hold his managers accountable for its support. As a result, whatever I told the staff went in one ear and out the other.

Without success, I pushed and pushed for six months. The staff seemed to like the training in principle, but no one made an effort to put the skills into practice, and there was no reinforcement from the owner or his leadership team to motivate people to change their behavior. After six months, I packed my bags and left with my tail between my legs.

It didn't take me long to realize what I had done wrong: I had not made it absolutely clear to the owner that none of the ECS and radical hospitality principles work in the absence of an owner's support; without active leadership, the process was doomed. It was that simple. I had assumed that he would be on board with the process and committed to making it work because he was paying me, but that wasn't the case. It is one of the most important lessons I've learned.

My experience at the SHC stands in stark contrast. True, at first not everyone was on board with the ECS program. In

142 ◆ EMOTIONAL EQUITY

fact, it's fair to say that several of the managers and more than a few of the frontline staff were hoping I would go away and take ECS with me. There were new systems to learn, more meetings, training sessions to attend, and much more monitoring of staff. Many people saw the soft skills at the heart of ECS as a burden, not a necessity. At first the ambivalence was subtle, but over time some of the SHC's managers started to push back against ECS. Everyone was busy and working hard to do their jobs, and some people felt they didn't have the ability to do more than they already were. They would tell me that their guests loved them and their staff, and they really didn't need to do anything else. They mocked the program as "touchy-feely stuff."

Dale and Stuart were aware of the pushback, thanks to their constant attention and insistence on maintaining open channels of communication throughout the organization. When the pushback reached a point where a critical mass of managers was openly opposing ECS, Dale and Stuart realized it was a make-or-break moment: Either they were going to agree that ECS was a bunch of hooey, or they were going "all in" to support the program. They chose the latter.

Dale and Stuart called a meeting with the management team to discuss the ECS program and the managers' concerns. "I know some of you feel ECS is an unnecessary burden and you don't buy in to it," Dale began. Several of the managers nodded. It was clear that they hoped he was about give them permission to bow out.

Dale continued: "Let me tell you that this is not an option. We are doing this full force, and if you aren't on board, you aren't going to be a good fit here."

Expressions of hope turned to shock. While both Dale and Stuart were great listeners, they were also decisive leaders. When they decided something was the right course of action, they committed to it and made sure it happened.

The room was quiet as Dale went on to explain in precise detail what ECS required of the managers. And he didn't stop there. Behind the scenes, he went to any manager who was resistant and had a talk with them. Not only that, at some point Dale and Stuart came to every department meeting and delivered the same message to the front lines: The ECS program was important, the SHC's leaders believed in it, it was here to stay, and everyone was responsible for making it work.

Dale and Stuart's intervention didn't turn the situation around immediately—that would have been an unrealistic expectation— ECS is as much about culture as individual behavior, and both things take time to change. But it was the consistent commitment of the SHC's leaders and their refusal to accept anything other than their staff's total cooperation that made the program work in the long run. Dale and Stuart and the Executive Committee made it clear what they expected, and they backed those expectations by holding people accountable, just as they did with every other principle of Emotional Equity.

Any organization that aspires to achieve what the SHC did requires the same level of commitment from its owners and executive leaders. Emotional Equity starts at the top. Without 100 percent backing, the process will fail.

CREATING RADICAL HOSPITALITY IN YOUR ORGANIZATION

When the corporation that bought the SHC in 2013 entered the picture, they made a big deal about the customer service program they use in all their hotels. They presented catchy slogans and shiny handouts, but its program didn't provide training, and it didn't have any systems to help the staff succeed in implementing it, or to ensure accountability, or to track and reward progress. No more magic wands for the staff, no more surprise and delight for the guests. Every penny spent or random act of kindness needed to be approved first. It took away the creativity, spontaneity and authenticity of the customer service; the personal touch was gone, and so was the special feeling that had set the SHC apart from its competitors.

That's what not to do. Here are the practices that any organization can use to create radical hospitality:

1. *Treat your staff the way you want them to treat your customers.* This builds directly on the culture of care. You set the tone for how your employees are expected to treat your customers by the way you treat them. Lead by example. People who feel cared for will go out of their way to care for others.

2. *Create a customer service program, not just a training.* An effective program starts with training to introduce key concepts and gets everyone speaking the same language, but training is just the beginning. Use the eight components of the Exceptional Customer Service program described in this chapter as a template. You might not be able to implement all of them, but the more you can put into practice, the more they will help reinforce what you expect from your staff. Regular meetings and following up with all guest feedback are two of the most critical points. These are detail-oriented practices, and, as Dale used to remind us, the details are often what separate success from failure.

3. *Make your customer service training more meaningful with the "Life Happiness Approach."* At first it may seem hokey to frame your customer service training as a matter of life happiness; but the fact is, customer service skills are

relationship skills that people can use in every facet of their lives. The key is helping your employees recognize that they will benefit from learning these skills. People are motivated by self-interest; we all want something if we think it is going to provide more pleasure. The Life Happiness Approach makes the connection between your customer service training and everyday life explicit. Practicing better relationship skills isn't something your employees are doing for you; it's something they are doing for themselves.

4. ***Get involved with your local community in meaningful ways.*** Find events to support, and more importantly, get your managers and frontline staff involved in activities and causes that enhance the community. Maybe you won't be the community's sweetheart, but you'll make connections and build relationships, which is good both for the heart of your business, and your bottom line.

5. ***Make sure the leader is committed to radical hospitality and willing to stand behind the program.*** If you are the leader, get ready to deal with some pushback. You need to make it absolutely clear that this is a priority, you are committed to it, and you will hold people accountable for making the program a success. It is better not to embark on this program at all if you aren't willing and able to back it 100 percent.

If you aren't the leader, make sure you have a clear commitment you can trust from the powers that be before you launch the program.

PRINCIPLE 7:
PROVIDE VALUE FOR MONEY

AROUND 2010, THERE WAS A SIGNIFICANT SHIFT in the hospitality industry: Private real estate investment trusts began purchasing hotels and hiring large management companies to run them. Individually owned hotels were giving way to global corporations, whose priority was generating high rates of return for their shareholders. The unspoken mantra was, "Make as much money as you can so that you can sell it for as much money as you can."

The mantra worked, at least in the short term. Massive increases in nightly rates, parking fees, and miscellaneous fees yielded astronomical profits. In 2016, *USA Today* reported that resort fees nationwide had increased 9 percent in the past year to $19.74 per night, with resorts in Key West charging some of the highest fees in the U.S., on average between $20 to $30 per night. Coupled with an ever-growing tourism industry in the

Keys, these fees helped the real estate investment trusts quickly boost profits.

Ultimately, the growth based on rate increases and fees was not sustainable. The bubble didn't burst as it did with the housing market; it slowly deflated. Too many competitors flooded the market, driving down average daily rates, and consumers fought back against the proliferation of fees. Guests complained so bitterly that in 2016 the Federal Trade Commission embarked on a process that would eventually require hotels to state their entire prices up-front.

Beginning in 2015, the increases to average daily rates in the Keys slowed down as occupancy began to decrease. In response, the pendulum swung the other way. A few choice hotels began distinguishing themselves from their competitors by doing away with extra fees. Many of my clients began talking about how to provide better service and give more to guests as a way to stand out in an overcrowded market. Key West's two top-ranked hotels on TripAdvisor became branded for giving great value. Their full prices were stated up-front, they had no parking or resort fees, they offered a fresh complimentary breakfast, other free amenities, and provided snacks and drinks around the pool gratis.

In the end, the focus on increasing profits through additional fees and massive rate increases sacrificed customer and employee happiness for dollars. It's a short-sighted approach, because it ignores the symbiotic relationship between customer satisfaction, staff morale, and profitability. It's hard for guests to enjoy even the most beautiful property and amenities when they feel duped from the first moment they arrive. Dissatisfied guests give the frontline staff a piece of their minds, who in turn lose heart. No one is engaged, and over time that impacts the bottom line.

Dale and Stuart knew this intuitively. They were shrewd businessmen who paid close attention to market trends, but they never followed practices that would upset their customers. They flat-out refused to charge resort and parking fees, even when their major competitors began to do it. Dale's retort to the idea was always the same: "If you go in like a pig, you're likely to come out like a sausage." He and Stuart simply refused to price-gouge or compromise on quality; they were focused on providing value. "We wanted to be up-front and straightforward with our guests," Stuart explains. "They got what they paid for and more."

This approach, combined with the resort's commitment to providing radical hospitality, earned the SHC loyal guests, consistent new business, a proud staff that stayed with the company for years, and phenomenal long-term financial results.

"Value for money was the driving force," explains Adelheid. "We never went for every last cent from our guests. We didn't charge for parking, Wi-Fi, or activities. We offered wonderful amenities, and we gave them great drinks and food at fair prices. Our guests came back every year, and they told all their friends about us. It brought us a great reputation and a lot of business."

Value for money wasn't just about room rates, amenities, and a refusal to charge hidden fees; it was about the total customer experience. Stuart often told staff, "We aren't a five-star hotel, but I want every person who stays here to feel like it is."

Four important factors defined the value for money approach at the SHC: The first was what Dale called "being beyond reproach"; the second was favoring long-term profitability over short-term gains; the third was meticulous budgeting; and the fourth was up-leveling staff. These principles aren't cutting edge. In fact, they are the opposite: "old-school" principles based on the simple notion that the best path to profitability is to offer a superior product and charge fairly for it.

MAKE YOUR BUSINESS "BEYOND REPROACH"

Rhonda the bartender often said she had been at the SHC for longer than she could remember. I always thought she was pretending to forget the number of years so no one could guess her age. According to her, she had been bartending "all her life." She could pretty much make your drink before you even ordered it, and she was always cheerful and friendly with guests.

But the day I met her, she was in a foul mood: Dale and Stuart, I would soon learn, had decided to tear down the dated tiki bar and build a new one twice the size, with a contemporary design and a mini prep kitchen for food.

When Rhonda learned that my job was helping the SHC improve its customer satisfaction, her piercing blue eyes lit up. Maybe I would be the person to champion her cause and help her save the old bar.

"Look at this," she said, waving her hand over the beat-up bar top like she was showing off a classic car. "Guests love this bar. It's got personality. It's Keysie and fun. It's not fancy-shmancy. And I'm telling you—that's what our guests like." She went on to complain at length about the plans for the new bar. The prep kitchen especially bothered her; making food, she argued, was something "real" bartenders didn't do.

Despite Rhonda's objections, Dale and Stuart moved forward with the renovation. They understood that many guests were okay with the bar the way it was, but they weren't content for any part of the SHC to simply be "good enough"; their goal was to always be beyond reproach. If even one customer was disappointed, there was room for improvement. As Dale often told the staff, products and services were only as good as the last customer's experience of them.

The tiki hut was replaced with a stunning, ultra-modern bar that had room for multiple bartenders and was equipped with the newest technology. Much to Rhonda's surprise, the hotel guests loved it, and the new edition attracted locals who started coming to the hotel for happy hour so they could relax and enjoy the upscale vibe after work. Once she started seeing her tip jar fill up faster than before, Rhonda softened. Soon after the new bar opened, she confided in me that it brought her more business.

The remodeled bar is only one example of the proactive, beyond-reproach philosophy Dale and Stuart had when it came to maintaining and improving the SHC. They never waited for guests to complain. Instead, they were always looking for opportunities to upgrade the property or add amenities. They didn't hesitate to make capital improvements if they thought the project would improve the guest experience. When they made renovations, they didn't cut corners. This commitment to quality made a positive impression on the staff and created a sense of pride throughout the organization.

"We were so happy to have a 100-percent product," says Front Desk Supervisor Wally Temple. "We actually wondered how anyone couldn't love the hotel. It felt great to give our guests the keys and know that it was going to be even more than they expected."

Shortly after they finished remodeling the bar, Dale and Stuart embarked on a series of major capital improvements that steadily transformed every part of the SHC over the course of several years, including the expansion of the Southernmost on the Beach and a complete upgrade of every room on the "dry side" of the hotel. They renovated the pool area, expanded the lobby, and re-landscaped the entire property.

"We didn't want one side of the resort dragging the other down," says Stuart. "At the time, the difference was great between the beach side and non-beach side properties. We needed the entire property to be a first-class operation, even if there were varying price levels for guests." Stuart's point was especially important in the era of social media reviews. "When someone reads a review about a shabby room on TripAdvisor, they don't know where on property the room is located," says Dale. "We needed every room to be fantastic."

As the capital improvements progressed, the SHC steadily moved up to its all-time high on TripAdvisor for the first time—number one. There were congratulatory emails, high-fives, hugs, and celebrations in every department. Occupancy rates increased from 2010 to 2011 by 9 percent, and revenue increased by more than $3 million.

Dale and Stuart expected their services to be beyond reproach, too. They hired an Activities team to keep families entertained throughout the day. They brought in musicians to play around the pool, and offered a "sunset celebration" over-looking the ocean. They rebuilt one of their pools to create a "tranquility area" for guests who wanted serenity and quiet. They ensured that their Guest Relations department left surprise champagne, chocolates, and personalized notes for every guest who was celebrating a special occasion. They maintained the rooms to perfection by replacing and refurbishing furniture regularly. Dale himself ensured that the drinks had a generous pour and were priced fairly. They brought in bar and lunch service to the pool areas so that guests never even had to leave their chairs.

I took on a client several years later that followed the SHC's example of being beyond reproach. The client, the Silver Palms

Inn, was a smaller hotel located in Old Town Key West. The inn had few amenities and a small pool, and it was not close to the beach. But none of these things prevented them from increasing the quality of their services to provide a better experience and greater value. They began treating guests to a complimentary drink at the bar after check-in and offering a number of free poolside services during the day (popsicles, cold face-towels, ice cream sundaes), complimentary water, and even an omelet station at breakfast. They started the ECS program, and really connected with their guests. Within a year, they rose to number 8 on TripAdvisor, a feat that exceeded even their own goals.

"When I was in Key West, I rarely ever left the property, even though it was right on Duval Street where all the action was," says longtime guest Stephen Lane. "We drank at the pool bars and ate at the café. There was no need to do anything else. The place was fantastic. My family has owned a lot of businesses, and these guys got it 100 percent right!"

The desire to get it "100 percent right" extended to the Southernmost Beach Café as well. In 2004, years before Dale and Stuart owned the restaurant, my husband and I had hosted a brunch there the day after our wedding. The food and the service were so disappointing that I decided never to step foot in the place again. The only thing the restaurant had going for it in those days was the view.

Five years later, Dale and Stuart asked me to meet them at the Café for lunch. Remembering the food at my wedding brunch, I ate lunch at home before heading to the restaurant. When I arrived, I was sorry I did. The place was packed and bustling. Wonderful smells wafted from the kitchen. The staff moved happily and quickly from one table to the next.

"What the heck happened here?" I wondered.

Dale and Stuart explained the improvements they had made. When they got ahold of it, the restaurant had offered the same menu for both lunch and dinner, there were few wine choices, and the quality of the food was subpar, as I had experienced. Instead of making incremental improvements, Dale and Stuart changed everything. They built a state-of-the art wine cooler with one of the largest selections on the island; introduced a new dinner menu to attract hotel guests and locals; and launched a killer happy-hour deal called 3 for $5, where guests could order any three fresh and "Keysie" appetizers for $5 each. It was a smash hit.

Most importantly, there was no more skimping on quality. They stopped incentivizing the restaurant's general manager for cutting food and labor costs. They made sure that the fish was fresh, and the steaks were top of the line. They increased prices to a level that supported the high-quality food and service but still felt fair to customers. The goal, as always, was to make the business be beyond reproach, which it most certainly was by the time I experienced it again. The results were reflected on the balance sheet, too: The restaurant went from losing money to a $6-million-per-year operation bringing close to $1 million to the bottom line.

Being beyond reproach is a strategy. While the tactics necessary to achieve the strategy will vary from business to business and industry to industry, it always starts with the same mindset. This mindset is based on the belief that the majority of consumers are savvy, they know quality when they see it, and they are willing to pay for quality if they know they are getting value for their money. I have heard many leaders claim that they go "above and beyond" for their customers, but when I see them price-gouge for a flimsy product, their words ring hollow. In contrast, Dale and Stuart were truly committed to giving the SHC's customers an authentically excellent experience at a fair price. They made their business beyond reproach, and they were rewarded by this philosophy.

FAVOR LONG-TERM PROFITABILITY

Flipping a business, like flipping houses, can be lucrative, but the short-term approach undermines the very notion of Emotional Equity. If the goal is to make as much money as you can in a short period of time and then sell, there is no opportunity or incentive to focus on people. The problem with this approach is that the short-term profits come at the expense of the business' long-term success, which requires a fundamental commitment to doing what is right for your employees and customers. I have seen many businesses suffer from a short-term mindset with an eye focused only on the bottom line. Things are shoddy, repairs are flimsy, and there is no real investment in relationships with staff or customers.

From the day they took over management of the SHC, Dale and Stuart were committed to building long-term value, instead of chasing short-term gains. It was this long-term thinking that made it possible for them to invest time and effort into Emotional Equity, instead of focusing exclusively on quick profits.

While they saw the SHC as a long-term investment, they never lost sight of the daily finances and their impact on the bottom line. At any given moment, Dale seemed to know the most recent profit and loss statement of every department off the top of his head. Both he and Stuart are numbers guys, but in a way I haven't encountered before. They were always aware of what the business was spending, but they didn't nickel-and-dime their managers—they refused to be bean counters.

This dichotomy confused me. How could they know the budget inside and out and scrutinize it daily without micromanaging it?

The answer is, they made almost every financial decision with the goal of long-term profitability in mind.

"Our focus was never to get the last dollar off the table," says Stuart. "Our definition of success was having the happiest guests on the island, and a long-term, stable, growing business."

That approach started with the way they capitalized the business. Stuart and Dale made sure with the SHC (and all of their business ventures) that it was not their only income stream. They counted on returns, but did not rely on them to pay their mortgages or put food on the table. That freed up capital for the business to make long-term investments in everything from staff to bricks and mortar.

"Many small businesses suffer from the needs of owners," explains Dale. "The way around it is that your standard of living cannot drive your actions for that business. Long-term value has to be the goal."

Dale and Stuart's ideology was antithetical to that of Sig Blum, the former managing partner who ran the SHC from 1985 until 2000. Sig's approach prefigured the one that big corporations and real estate trusts would adopt two decades later—generate as much short-term profit as you can, no matter the long-term consequences. Sig's results were similar, too. Guests were frustrated, staff turnover was high, and customers were dissatisfied. The only people who benefited were the investors.

When Stuart and Dale took over the SHC, they immediately began to shift the focus of the business. Meeting annual distribution targets was no longer the top priority. "We made the decision that we were going to change course," explains Stuart.

"We paid very close attention to details and tried to eliminate the negatives one by one. Our aim was growth and value."

As a result, the staff and the resort itself started to come to life. More resumes came in from people who heard about the changing culture at the SHC and wanted to work there. The base of loyal, repeat guests that Matt and Carrie had worked so hard to build through the '80s and '90s started to grow. Guest satisfaction steadily improved. The practices of Emotional Equity took root and flourished. And with each change Dale and Stuart implemented, the SHC became more profitable.

The transformation from Sig's bottom-line focus to Emotional Equity didn't happen overnight, of course, and the SHC still had to contend with the same shocks to the broader economy that other businesses did. For example, early in Dale and Stuart's leadership tenure, tourism slowed globally after the terrorist attacks of September 11, 2001. Many people stopped getting on planes for travel, and workers in the hospitality sector across the U.S. feared for their jobs. Key West was no exception.

With occupancy down in the months following the terrorist attacks, Dale gathered the SHC's entire management team to address the crisis. Layoffs were happening all over the island, and other resorts were slashing rates in an attempt to get heads on beds. The obvious short-term solution would have been for the SHC to follow suit. The managers were expecting the worst. Instead, Dale announced that the SHC would not be laying off any staff. He had also decided not to deeply discount rates, since it wouldn't do anything for short-term occupancy, and he didn't want to overreact with respect to the coming season's rates. Despite being in rough waters and not knowing when calm would return, he refused to abandon his principles in favor of short-term thinking that only would have caused more problems in the long run.

The SHC survived the difficult 2001–2002 tourism season, and was well positioned to prosper once the travel industry began to recover.

Years later, when the hotel sold for a record-breaking $184.5 million, I asked Dale if he ever secretly questioned himself during the difficult period in the early 2000s. His answer: "I didn't know what was going to happen, but I assure you I wouldn't have changed a thing."

Dale's confidence in Emotional Equity and its long-term approach is well founded and backed up by the returns on investment the SHC produced under his and Stuart's leadership. After 2001, they distributed a minimum of $325,000 annually, split 50–50 between the investors and the general partners; in some years they distributed more than $2 million. In the end, Dale and Stuart's commitment to long-term value and Emotional Equity yielded a 40-percent internal rate of return for them and their investors.

BE METICULOUS IN YOUR BUDGETING

To an outsider looking in on the SHC, it could have seemed that Dale and Stuart were big spenders. If they wanted to hire a great candidate for a bit more money than they had planned, they did it. If the innkeeper at the guesthouses said she needed new tableware, they gave her the freedom to go out that same day and buy it. If there was a need to increase payroll by adding positions, such as additional pool attendants and guest relations staff, they added the new positions. When they purchased furniture for the new lobby and renovated rooms, it was top of the line. Staff would secretly take bets on what the next big capital improvement project would be. Another new addition? A new pool? Mini-golf? There was always a buzz of curiosity about what was around the corner.

It's true that Dale and Stuart were willing to spend on capital improvements, maintenance, and their staff, but they were never reckless. In fact, they were meticulous in their financial planning, but in a way that didn't prevent them or their managers from being flexible when the need arose. Much of this flexibility came from the budgeting process.

When Dale and Stuart took over the SHC, they did away with the typical budgeting process used by most businesses. Many organizations look at the previous year's budgets and make projections for the following year by simply adding the inflation factor. In contrast, Dale and Stuart used a system of zero-based budgeting. They started the budget from scratch every year, and calculated the cost of every line item by checking prices with their vendors and providers. They did the same with revenue. It was a clean slate every time.

"My partners would occasionally ask me how our expenses were tracking compared to the previous year," says Dale. "My answer was in so many words, 'I do not know offhand, and I don't really care.' I cared about meeting our current budgets and maintaining or increasing our profit margins."

As part of the process, each department head was responsible for submitting a budget for all expense categories within their department, accompanied by a detailed list of where they were spending the money. Each utility provider was contacted and asked about future rate increases, ensuring that all bases were covered. Underlying data for each line item in the income statement was detailed. Major expenses such as insurance and taxes were budgeted based upon projected revenue, income and payroll increases. No stone was left unturned. When revenue increased, they expected and allowed for an increase in expenses for products and staffing needs. For example, between 2010 and

2013, revenues and occupancies were exceeding budget; and as a result, certain expenses such as utilities, housekeeping, and maintenance had increased as well. These increased expenditures weren't a cause for concern, because they were understood to be a natural consequence of growth, and they were already accounted for in the budgeting process.

In addition to annual budgets per department, the Executive Committee prepared three- to five-year capital improvement budgets by project that included substantial funds for miscellaneous replacements. These capital improvement budgets gave them the freedom to spend money when unexpected situations arose.

Despite such detailed processes, the budget was always treated as a guideline, not a sacred text. There were always line-item variances, many of them due to timing of when expenditures were made during the year. For example, if a large purchase for housekeeping supplies was made in April that had been budgeted for May, there was a variance, but it didn't negatively affect the overall budget.

"Many companies require each manager to prepare a monthly report explaining any line item that varies from budget by more than 2 or 3 percent," says Dale. "That's a big waste of time. Do I really want to know why a $3,000 item was $150 over budget? No. But if payroll was over budget, I wanted to know why. I asked accounting to point out variances and asked the department head to explain the reasons. If I was not satisfied with the explanation, I made further inquiry."

The process of zero-based budgeting was time-consuming, and it could sometimes be tedious; but in the long run it helped the SHC's leaders meet and exceed their financial goals year after year. It enabled them to accurately anticipate and track the resort's costs, while at the same time providing them the flexibility to deal with the unexpected expenses that regularly materialize in the hospitality industry. It also empowered their managers to make smaller purchases quickly and efficiently, which freed the Executive Committee to focus their attention on bigger issues, like capital improvements and growing the business.

UP-LEVEL YOUR STAFF

In 2008, when Dale, Stuart and their partners purchased the famous Atlantic Shores Hotel, the SHC went from a three-star, mostly land-side property to a four-star resort with oceanfront rooms. Guests on the ocean side were paying premium rates to enjoy the new property, and they expected the excellent service received. A "Hey, howya doin?" mom-and-pop approach at check-in was no longer adequate. More importantly, Dale and Stuart recognized there was an opportunity for more revenue on the horizon. With the newly acquired property's beautiful pool, beach sundeck, bar, and spa, they could now offer a true resort experience that would keep guests around the pools, eating and drinking all day. If they could get it right, guests would spend their money at the resort instead of elsewhere on the island. That meant the SHC's service needed to be top-notch.

"At that time, we got clear that our goal was to give five-star service at affordable rates," recalls Stuart. "That was what set us apart from our competition."

Stuart's insight into the value of high-end service was right on the money—literally. Service matters to customers as much, if not more, than product. According to a 2014 report in *Harvard Business Review*, customers who enjoy a business' service spend on average 140 percent more money there.

Dale and Stuart knew it would take a concerted effort to raise the SHC to a higher level of service. "Many of our staff had not experienced five-star service and didn't know what it looked like," says Stuart. "We could talk about it all we wanted, but they really needed to see it for themselves." So instead of issuing a few memos about the need for staff to be more professional and provide better service to guests, the Executive Committee introduced two initiatives designed to up-level their employees. First, they sent key staff members to secret-shop five-star hotels and high-end restaurants throughout South Florida. They used this feedback to incorporate new practices into their own service. Second, they committed resources and their unwavering support to the creation and implementation of the Exceptional Customer Service Program described in Principle 6: Radical Hospitality, which became an integral part of the SHC's culture.

The secret shopping missions were a great perk for the managers who enjoyed these excursions, and they brought back valuable insights that helped make the SHC's operations more sophisticated. Matt sent his restaurant manager and chef to Key West restaurants with top ratings on TripAdvisor. Dale and Stuart sent the SHC's bar manager to the Breakers, one of the finest hotels in Florida; and they sent the pool manager to the Casa Marina, the oldest and finest hotel in Key West. Adelheid herself secret-shopped the Ritz Carlton. All of them came back with energy, enthusiasm, and fresh ideas.

It was a big boost for staff to see the execution of their ideas. For example, after his trip, the pool manager decided that his team needed to provide more perks to make the guests feel special. The pool attendants began handing out frozen face-towels soaked in eucalyptus oil; they offered guests complementary frozen fruit pops; and they brought around trays of ice water. These were simple and inexpensive initiatives, but guests felt appreciated and raved about them on social media. That was precisely what the Executive Committee envisioned, knowing that the little things often make the biggest difference.

The focus on service paid off: As the SHC's level of service improved to match its amenities, guests who had previously used the hotel as a launching pad to do other things in Key West began staying at the resort all day and evening, just as the Executive Committee had designed.

"Our service was what guests loved about us most," explains Shores Bar server, Heather Kelly. "They would actually tell me they loved the vibe with the staff, and would rather be with us than on Duval Street. We made them feel special, and we did it in a real and genuine way."

Real and genuine service made all the difference. That was the focus of the ECS program, and what I repeated again and again in training sessions with frontline staff and in leadership coaching with managers. I've often found the service at five-star hotels to be uptight and stiff, though never lacking courtesy and professionalism. Uptight and stiff isn't the Key West vibe, and it wasn't what the guests wanted at the SHC; they wanted five-star courtesy and professionalism with genuine warmth and a personal touch. So that's what we focused on providing.

With this commitment to service, the SHC became branded for giving their guests value for their money in every possible way. Sending their staff on secret shopping missions and creating and sustaining the ECS program cost far less than the major capital improvements that inspired them, and yet these efforts to up-level the staff were equally important to the SHC's long-term success.

HOW TO PROVIDE MORE VALUE FOR MONEY
IN YOUR ORGANIZATION

Price, as the saying goes, is only an issue in the absence of value. This applies to every business in every industry, and at every price point from low to high. Most people know when they're getting good value and when they're not, and they choose where to spend their money accordingly. The leaders of the SHC understood this as a guiding principle.

Regardless of what your business is, you want your customers to feel they're getting what they paid for, and more. Four practices from the SHC can help:

1. **Give your total price up-front.** Hidden fees may yield more profit in the short term, but over time they will cost you customers. Instead of charging extra fees, as their competitors were doing, the SHC simply raised its rates and advertised that it was the full price guests would pay, with no additional charges. As a result, occupancy and repeat business increased. The SHC made as much money as their competitors in the long run (and eventually more), but they did it in a way that didn't make customers feel misled or cheated.

2. **Stand out by offering unexpected or unique perks to customers.** It astounded me to see how often guests at the SHC would mention the frozen face-towels and free popsicles at the pool in their survey responses. In the grand scheme of business, these were small gestures with significantly positive impact on the guests' experiences. Unexpected perks, even if they are small, can make a big impression.

3. **Make your service and products beyond reproach.** That means up-leveling your people through training in leadership and customer service on a consistent basis, and constantly

looking at your business with scrutiny to evaluate how your products can be improved based on your budget.

4. *Know your budget inside and out, but don't let your budget dictate every spending decision.* This is a delicate balance. It requires highly detailed, accurate planning and monitoring, as well as an allowance for a sizable miscellaneous category that provides flexibility to respond to unforeseen issues and opportunities. If a great candidate walks through the door, you want to have room in your budget to make the hire. If something needs replacing, it should happen quickly without tangling your managers in red tape.

PART III

PUTTING EMOTIONAL EQUITY TO WORK IN YOUR ORGANIZATION

BRIDGING THE GAP BETWEEN THEORY AND PRACTICE

IT'S EASY FOR LEADERS TO SAY THEY'RE ON BOARD with the philosophy of being good to their people. But talking about Emotional Equity and actually putting it into practice are different.

When I introduce the seven principles of Emotional Equity to a new client, I almost always get a resounding "amen." Most leaders nod emphatically in agreement as I cite examples to illustrate the benefits that will arise from empowering people, genuine relationship-building, providing value for money, and taking great care of their customers. "We're doing a lot of these things already," they tell me.

But once I step out of the executive office and meet the front-line staff, I hear a different story. More often than not, morale is low, people are in conflict with each other, and very few staff members feel truly committed or loyal to the job or their leaders. It's not uncommon for people on the front lines to tell me point-blank, "No one at the top cares about us."

The gap between what leaders think they are doing and how they are perceived is the biggest reason organizations fail to build Emotional Equity. Most leaders honestly believe they are putting their people first, but in truth they rarely go beyond superficial benchmarks like annual employee surveys. As a result, they lack a genuine understanding of what their people think and feel. When I reveal that their staff are unhappy, they are shocked. Confronting this reality is not easy. Some leaders get defensive and cling to the status quo. These leaders might be committed to Emotional Equity in theory, but they never achieve it in practice. Other leaders are inspired to take action and close the gap.

If you genuinely want to build Emotional Equity in your orga-nization, the seven principles must be practiced. In the preceding chapters, I concluded my discussion of each principle with a few suggestions for execution. These suggestions are most helpful if you have already identified which principle(s) you want to work on. But what if you're not sure where to begin?

As the final takeaway of this book, I offer the framework I use to help my clients get started with Emotional Equity. The frame-work is simple: Start by asking your employees and customers for their honest opinions on the strengths and weaknesses of your organization, then use that feedback to identify the most important problem you need to address. Once you know what that problem is, check the lists below to find the corresponding Emotional Equity principle that will help you solve it. Finally, choose one or more of the recommended actions to focus on, and begin putting the principle into practice.

THE FIRST STEP IN BUILDING EMOTIONAL EQUITY: MINE FOR INPUT

Emotional Equity begins with relentless inquiry. It's not enough to listen when employees and customers come to you with issues or suggestions; you need to go out and mine for input.

At the SHC, Dale and Stuart and the Executive Committee were always mining for input. Through formal channels they used annual surveys and HR to gather employee feedback, but the most useful information they learned always came from face-to-face communication. The SHC's leaders talked to their managers, front lines, and guests on a daily basis, and they constantly (and I mean *constantly*) asked questions. Sometimes they would ask open-ended questions like "How are things going here?" But more often they asked pointed, specific questions focused on the details of the operation. The goal was to know what was working and what wasn't, and to understand why.

When Dale and Stuart began the practice of mining for input, the staff were surprised to be asked for their opinions, and many people were reluctant to answer honestly. If the leaders sensed hesitation or uncertainty, they delved deeper and reassured the staff that they needed their honest input. They persisted until they felt they got a genuine response.

At the same time, the SHC's leaders were careful not to let this discourse turn into a "whiner culture" in which employees felt entitled to anything they asked for. If Dale and Stuart and the Executive Committee members felt someone was complaining without offering constructive ideas, they addressed that person directly and made clear that they were looking for solutions, not only problems. They also made it clear that just because they were seeking input from the staff, it didn't mean they were going to do everything that was asked of them. There was no doubt in anyone's mind that their leaders reserved the right to make a decision.

The key to making this type of inquiry productive is to consistently follow up on the feedback received. If the SHC's leaders felt there was a valid concern that needed to be addressed, they took action. If they decided not to make a change, they got back to the person who raised the concern to explain why.

The best way to mine for input is to take a few minutes every day (or as often as you can) to walk around your organization and talk to your staff and customers. Ask questions and really listen to what people have to say. When you get an answer you don't fully understand, dig deeper. Ask for examples. Resist the urge to argue or shut down ideas. Take notes and follow up for clarification when necessary. Remind your people that you might not do what they are asking, but assure them that you will always close the communication loop and explain your decisions.

When getting started with Emotional Equity, make mining for input a top priority for two weeks. During this time, talk individually and informally with as many customers and members of your team as you can. At the end of the two weeks, analyze the feedback you have collected and match the negative feedback to the common problems listed below. Whichever Emotional Equity principle has the most negative feedback associated with it is where to begin. Make it your goal for the next month to adopt some of the actions that correspond with that principle. There are many actions to choose, and often a little bit goes a long way.

Problems: Feelings that the culture is stale; lack of solid and knowledgeable staff; low morale; pervasive negativity amongst co-workers; lack of teamwork.

Principle 1: Get the "A Team" On Board

1. Poach great personalities. Don't sit around waiting for good people to answer your help-wanted ads. Be on the lookout every day for the type of personality you want to attract to your business. Ask managers and frontline staff to do the same. If you think the checkout person at the grocery store is exceptionally warm and friendly, give them your business card and tell them to call you. Better yet, ask for their phone number so that you can follow up instead of waiting for them to call. Try to find at least one potential person per week. A finder's fee can be a great incentive for this at all levels of the organization.

2. Bring on two or three people who have worked for you in the past and put them in key leadership positions (including middle management). This doesn't mean hiring a personal friend, but rather someone with whom you have worked in the past and admired. Don't speculate in advance about reasons they might not take the job. You won't know until you ask.

3. Make a list of the personality traits you want in each managerial position in your company. If it's the head of customer service, you'll want a winning, warm personality. If it's the director of operations, you'll want someone who is organized, calm and conscientious. Use these traits as key criteria when evaluating candidates. It's often tempting to choose the candidate who requires less technical training, but that is not necessarily the best choice for the long term. Without the right personality for the job, it won't matter how much they know,

and you will probably find yourself hiring for that position again sooner rather than later. (Remember that it costs 30 to 50 percent of an individual's salary to replace them.)

4. Review your salary scale to ensure that you pay slightly more than your competitors. While money isn't the only factor in the hiring equation, it is definitely important for attracting good candidates. Research your comp set every three to six months to make sure you are at the top of the game. There are many resources available, including annual wage and benefit surveys published by most Chambers of Commerce. It is also helpful to informally ask around with people you know at other organizations in your industry. Make sure that you don't start your compensation scale so high that you can't afford pay increases and/or bonuses at least on an annual basis.

5. Aim for an "A Team" that is about 20 percent of your workforce. This target represents a "critical mass" of carefully selected key people in each department and at different levels of your organization (in middle management on the front lines, especially) who set the tone and establish the culture for everyone else. Evaluate the staffing needs of each department through this lens. When a particular department isn't thriving, find a few "A Teamers" to place there to revive the energy.

6. Make your interviews conversational and relaxed. The goal is to observe the candidate's personality. Use at least four or five behavioral questions/case scenarios to see how they intuitively respond (e.g., "What would you do in this situation?"). Tap in to the candidate's background, interests and passions, and future goals. Use your gut to determine whether they seem authentic, and ask yourself if they have the personality you want for that position.

Problems: Lack of employee initiative; boredom; malaise; laziness; lack of innovation, spirit and creativity; the 9-to-5 mentality.

Principle 2: Empowerment

1. People need and want the opportunity to fix problems. Without that freedom, their morale suffers and eventually they become apathetic. Encourage staff to think of creative ideas for turning around unhappy customers, and thank them when they do it. Encourage them to think outside the box and have fun with it. If your business is hospitality, give your front lines "fun money" to spend on guests (or easy access to it).

2. Make changes quickly. If there is a policy or practice that is not working for your people, fix it. Whenever possible, cut out bureaucratic approval processes and get rid of procedures that require unnecessary paperwork or take too much time to complete. Ask yourself, "Is there a way to streamline this process?" If so, do it. Communicate to people directly when you make changes as a result of their feedback.

3. Review your employee policies and omit or change the ones that are built on mistrust. It is important to have reasonable checks and balances in place, but watching cameras all day or making punitive rules based on the misconduct of one employee incriminates the entire team and makes everyone feel that leadership does not trust them.

4. Give your front lines the authority to make decisions about how to handle unhappy customers without having to bring in management, unless it's a major issue. Remind them that you trust them, and give them the freedom to use their discretion. If you disagree with a particular decision, discuss it

with them privately, but not in a way that would shut down their ability to act independently in the future.

5. Dedicate time in your staff meetings to ask your staff to respond to tough and/or controversial questions about the business. Make sure you don't shut anyone down for giving input. If you are struggling with employee retention, ask your staff why people are leaving and what they think would solve the problem. If you are looking for ways to improve your product, ask your staff what they think about the product and what feedback they are hearing from customers. Whatever the topic, listen without giving your own input. Take the feedback and use it to guide your decisions with the understanding that you don't need to take the advice of your people, but you do need to listen to them. If your decision is different than the majority's feedback, go back to them and explain why.

Problems: Lack of follow-through; inconsistency; breaking rules; taking advantage of company policies and offerings that are mean to support and thank staff; insubordination.

Principle 3: Accountability

1. Use the "3 W's" (What, When and Why) to communicate directives. Clarity in communication is the first step in creating accountability. If staff can't understand what you want, it is unfair to hold them accountable for following through on it. To ensure that your message is received and understood, use the follow-up question "What's the plan?" and have people repeat back what they heard.

2. Inspect what you expect. Follow up on a consistent basis to make sure that people are doing what you have asked.

That does not mean micromanaging them. Rather, put in your calendar a reminder once a week to check on a new directive. Connect with staff periodically before deadlines to make sure they are clear on what they are responsible for delivering. Deadlines are most effective if you ask your staff to set them. That way people take ownership of the project and assign themselves a time to complete it that seems feasible to them. Once you establish a pattern of regular follow-ups, people will be more likely to perform their tasks consistently.

3. Create observation checklists. Choose a staff member every few days to observe. You can do this while you work with them, or as you do your own work. Don't make them feel uncomfortable, and it's not even necessary to let them know you are observing them (though you can do that, depending on the situation). When you have a quiet moment, talk with them alone and in private to review what they did well and what needs more work. If there were things missing, do another few observations in the coming days to make sure they are getting it right.

4. Create a formal feedback loop based on customer input. Make sure that someone (you or a point person in charge of customer relations) shares all relevant customer feedback— the good and the bad—on a daily basis with employees at all levels of the organization. If front lines are mentioned, their manager should share the information with them, and report back to the leader or point person. Key managers should be copied. For example, if a customer at a restaurant complains on social media that their server was rude, the point person should send this to the manager, who must then find out who it was, get the story and share it with the point person. This feedback loop helps ensure that problems are addressed, and it shows front lines that management will hold them

accountable for their actions. Likewise, if someone receives a positive mention, they should be rewarded and thanked by their manager and leaders.

5. Replace impersonal, institutionalized rewards with meaningful ones. Show your team appreciation for what they do in ways that are personal and authentic. Before you offer praise to a staff member, think of how to say in a way that will matter to them. Instead of "great job today," tell them what specifically you appreciated about what they did and how that impacts you, their colleagues, or the customer. Know what your staff members' hobbies, passions and interests are, and do something for them that is personalized. If you know they love their pets, buy them a gift certificate to the pet store. If they love sweets, buy them a small box of handmade chocolates. It doesn't have to be extravagant, just personally meaningful.

6. Address mistakes immediately and consistently. Be direct and specific, and start by focusing on the correct behavior that you want to see happen in the future. Use the 3 W's to make your expectations clear. Do this on the spot, if possible (though not in front of peers or customers). Ask the person to explain what happened. If there is no good reason for the mistake, take corrective action appropriate to the situation. When you decide to hold staff accountable for a specific practice, policy, procedure, or rule, you must be 100 percent consistent in your reinforcement of it. If you let someone slide even once, you start to lose credibility, and accountability becomes nearly impossible to achieve.

Problem: Infighting; negativity; silos; talking behind people's backs; bringing personal vendettas to work; accusations of favoritism; employees trying to get each other in trouble; gossip.

Principle 4: Manage and Resolve Conflicts

1. Build consensus, but don't let it drive your decisions. It is critical to get employee input, listen to their ideas, and delve in to their suggestions. At the same time, it is necessary to reserve the right to override decisions. When you choose to take a path that is different from the majority's requests, make sure you explain your decision and the rationale behind it.
2. Use curative coaching. When you know that you have a problem employee, get involved to see if the situation can be fixed with coaching rather than discipline. Take action by meeting with the person in private, talking with them about the situation and putting in writing concrete commitments/agreements to improve the situation. If, for example you have an employee who isn't pulling his weight, work with him to identify four or five very specific tasks he will commit to doing daily. Then monitor him weekly (for at least four weeks) to hold him accountable for those commitments.
3. Mediate between employees who are in conflict. Don't let it go, and don't dismiss the problem by telling them to "play nice"—this is ineffective at best and usually just makes the situation worse. If you don't have experience mediating conflicts, ask a qualified person in HR to get involved, or hire a consultant. You can also get trained as a mediator (there are short online courses that provide effective training). A successful mediation will result in specific, concrete agreements for which both parties will be held accountable and that will be monitored by a neutral third party (usually the mediator).
4. Treat employee complaints as seriously as you want your employees to treat customer complaints. Resist the urge to dismiss employee complaints, even if you think they are

whining. Listen to what your people have to say, ask clarifying questions and seek examples, and then check to see if the complaint is shared by others. Always allow yourself time to think about the issue before making a decision. If your answer to a request is no, explain why. They may not be happy, but at least they'll understand your reasoning.

5. Work with your mavericks. If you have an employee who is great at his job but marches to the beat of his own drum, ask yourself how you can work with him. If he causes too much chaos, he probably is not a good fit; but remember that most organizations benefit from the people who bring new ideas and different approaches to the table. Work with him privately to set limits or use curative coaching for a specified period of time (two months is usually sufficient). After that, determine if what you have done is working enough to keep him on board.

6. Make sure you always create written agreements and establish regular check-ins when taking corrective action, whether it be curative coaching or mediation. Without specific, concrete actions in place and consistent follow-up to ensure those actions are being taken, there can be no resolution to a problem. People can agree to disagree, but they have to live up to that agreement in everyday life. Conflicts are never resolved by having people air their grievances unless the talk is followed by a plan of action that both parties are held accountable for following through on.

7. Have your team read one book a year on communication skills. Choose a book that helps your team prevent conflict and work with each other and customers. Buy it for them and assign a set number of pages per month. Hold them accountable for reading the book by asking them to discuss

it at staff meetings. Some great ones to choose from include: *The Five Dysfunctions of a Team*, by Patrick Lencioni; *Good to Great*, by Jim Collins; *Emotional Intelligence*, by Daniel Goleman; and *Getting to Yes*, by Roger Fisher, William L. Ury, and Bruce Patton.

Problem: High turnover; lack of employee engagement; apathy; lack of loyalty to the company and to the leadership; complaints that things aren't fair; sentiments that all ownership/leadership care about is the bottom line.

Principle 5: A Culture of Care

1. Manage by Walking Around (MBWA). Walk around every day (or as often as you can) to build rapport and tap in to your staff and customers. Don't have an agenda for these interactions; let them be natural. Get to know people; ask about their jobs and their lives (without getting too personal). Take the opportunity to ask pointed questions about something specific to your business. Your goal is to build genuine relationships. This creates loyalty and helps you understand how to provide meaningful rewards for your staff, and it provides information and insights that you would never glean from formal surveys.

2. Remember important details. When you find out that something big is going on in your staff's lives, remember it and follow up with them. If someone they love is sick, make sure you ask about them and show you care. If they just went on a special vacation, inquire about it. Ask for the highlight.

3. Encourage your staff to show your customers how much they care, and let them do it in their own way. Remind them

all the time that their job is to create an experience and to connect with customers. That doesn't mean they should develop personal relationships with them (nor should you with your staff), but it does mean that you encourage them to go out of their way to "surprise and delight" customers. (See Principle 2: Empowerment.)

4. Look for spontaneous ways to show your people what they mean to you. Offer them your rain jacket if they are walking to the bus from work and it's pouring outside. If you see them at a restaurant, send them over a dessert or a drink from you. If they seem tired or distraught, ask if they are okay. Call them to check in on them if they are sick for a few days. Send flowers for a major occasion. Organize a baby shower. Small acts of kindness go a long way.

5. Offer help without being asked. If you know one of your staff members is going through a hard time, discuss internally what you can do for them. Find them a resource, pay for a service they might need, volunteer some of your time if you have it. Don't give more than you have, but reach out to your people in their deepest times of need, instead of waiting for them to ask you.

6. Create a program to support employee wellness that comes directly from your employees' interests. As you walk around daily and talk with your people and ask questions, find out how the organization could support them in their health and wellness. Do they want to run a group race? Do they want smoking cessation groups or Fitbits? Poll them to see what the majority are interested in. Then find a staff member or small group (task force) to head the efforts. Give them the power to organize the wellness program and decide how it should work. Participate by showing up to their meetings

and listening. Offer as much support as you can without leading the process.

7. Find at least one new way to help your people grow financially in the short or long term. If you can't offer stock options, consider other innovative ways of helping them benefit from years of working with you. Implement bonus programs, investment opportunities, or even offer financial planning classes that you pay for.

Problem: Low ratings on social media; negative reviews on guest surveys; losing business to competitors; an attitude of contempt towards customers from staff.

Principle 6: Radical Hospitality

1. Start a comprehensive program on customer service. A one-shot training is simply not enough to reinforce a culture of service. Sit down with your management team and decide on a multi-faceted program to instill the level of service your organization needs. You can outsource this to a company and/or do part of it yourself. Consider including at least the following components: (1) a standardized training for all new staff; (2) survey/social media goals; (3) monthly or quarterly meetings to review customer service skills and tools and teach new ones; and (4) secret-shopping the competition.

2. Make it a priority to reward Random Acts of Kindness. What matters to you will matter to your people. When you hear or see a staff member do something truly kind for a guest (or a co-worker), tell them what it means to you. Bring it up at management meetings as an example of what "sets us apart

from the rest." The more you talk about it, the more your staff will delight in doing it.

3. Train your managers to reinforce customer service. Your managers need to know what to expect of the front lines and how to make sure it is done well. Without consistent training and tools, reinforcing customer service is haphazard at best. The easiest tool to use is observation checklists to periodically provide feedback to staff on the skills and tools they need to know to provide great service. Also, make sure your managers pop-quiz their staff daily as they practice MBWA and at pre-shift meetings.

4. Choose a cause in your community. There is no better way to make sure that the local community knows and loves you than to adopt a cause and support it. When it's possible, say yes to nonprofits, schools, and events. Offer your space to support community initiatives and get your staff involved. As community members, they will benefit too. Even in this age of social media, word-of-mouth recommendations from people who know your company carry a great deal of weight and will bring you new customers.

5. Make sure the top leader is 100 percent on board with your efforts. When promoting customer service you should expect pushback from your staff at first, or worse, apathy. Most frontline staff are not excited about new programs that require them to change the way they do their jobs, and some don't feel that the training is necessary. When you get resistance, bring in the owner/CEO to talk to individuals and entire teams to let them know that they are expected to be an active part of the program.

6. Let your staff be themselves. Scripted service comes across as uptight, rote and disingenuous. Go into your next staff

meeting with the message that people should be the best versions of themselves with each other and the customers. Let them express who they are in their own way. Explain that there is no compromising graciousness, but how they express it is up to them.

Problem: Complaints from guests and staff about the product; staff who feel embarrassed or nervous about selling; the accusation that there is not "value for money" in your product and/or service.

Principle 7: Value for Money

1. Ask yourself: Is my business "beyond reproach"? When you start to make changes that might anger or upset the customer, ask yourself objectively if you feel you are beyond reproach from the consumer's perspective. We have all heard the rhetoric about seeing things from the "eyes of your customer," but being beyond reproach takes it to a new level.

2. Choose quality. Decisions on investment come up daily in your business. Whether it's major capital expenditures or deciding on a coffee machine your customers will use, choose quality. It's easy and tempting to go with a quick fix or something that looks good for a short while, but the opportunity cost of that choice is high. Aim for long-term quality and steady growth.

3. Give your staff consistent training and tools. People are a large part of your product. Invest in them the way you would your business. Look for fun and creative ways to grow your staff. Send them to other businesses to "secret-shop" and come back with new ideas; ask them what kinds of workshops

or seminars they want and arrange for it; and implement programs that provide ongoing and consistent training (not just a one-shot deal) on customer service.

4. Use zero-based budgeting. It is more labor- and time-intensive to take this approach, but it provides your business with a precise picture of its current finances and gives you an accurate guide for the future. Teach your managers to do it, and engage in the process annually.

5. Do not micromanage your budget. Public companies, whose primary focus is their stock price, often go overboard attempting to meet or exceed their budgets. When they are in jeopardy of failing to meet these projections, directives are issued requiring expense cuts across all departments. It is a meat-ax approach which often sacrifices long-term health to achieve short-term goals.

   Prior to the beginning of each fiscal year, prepare a monthly revenue and expenditure budget utilizing input from all department heads. Remember, however, that the budget is a projection and a guideline; it should not be the bible. There will always be variances. The important thing is to discover the reasons for the variances through proper investigation and reporting from the accounting department and for management to determine whether they are justifiable. For example, variances in expenditures are often due to timing difference between various months: Department heads will expend a budgeted amount a month earlier or later than forecasted in the budget. Variances in revenue may be due to factors beyond management's control. If there is a small variance in a relatively small line item in your budget, there is no need to nickel-and-dime your managers. Require explanations only when they are important.

CONCLUSION

I HAVE SHARED THE SHC'S STORY and the seven principles of
Emotional Equity with many clients all over the world in a variety
of circumstances, from Shiite and Sunni community leaders in
war-torn Iraq, to insurance companies in Miami and restaurant
owners in the Keys. When leaders commit to these ideas and
put them into practice, the change is quick and often extreme.
Organizations have a happier staff, they move up on social media,
they improve retention rates, and they increase profits.

Bridging the gap between understanding the principles of
Emotional Equity and putting them into practice is easier than it
might seem. Start with the framework outlined above: Mine for
input, identify an area where your organization needs to improve,
and choose a recommended action that addresses the issue at
hand. Then, once the first action is in place, choose two more
actions from the list and put them into practice too. Don't assume
that you have to implement every recommendation of the seven

principles at the same time, even if you agree with them. Start with the principle that relates to your most important needs, and build from there. As time goes by, expand to incorporate other principles. And if you already engage in some of the practices, remember that there is always room to get better and build more loyalty among your staff and customers.

The story of the SHC is one that can guide almost any company. It teaches us that building genuine relationships with staff and customers is good for business, and that investing in Emotional Equity leads to greater financial equity in the long term. To embrace the principles that Dale, Stuart, Matt, Carrie, and Adelheid put into practice at the SHC is to embrace the fact that human beings—customers and employees—are at the heart of every business, and that the greatest results come from focusing not only on making a good living, but on making a good life.

ACKNOWLEDGMENTS

FROM DALE RANDS AND STUART KAUFMAN

WE WOULD LIKE TO THANK:

Sig Blum for discovering the property and recognizing its potential, Mort Harris and Bill Berman for their confidence in us; Craig Singer for his invaluable contribution on our construction projects; Matt Babich and Carrie Babich for their twenty-five years of devoted on-site leadership and management; our entire management team for their diligence and loyalty, including but not limited to, Adelheid Salas (director of operations), Skip and Teresa Ross (director of engineering and controller), Monika Pearson and her predecessor June Morfi (executive head house-keepers), Megan Coccitto and her predecessor Lisa Malcolm (marketing directors), Lena Warner Scott (chief accountant), Rozsa Dimando (reservations and revenue manager), Duane Webster (IT manager); Todd Jones, Elizabeth Isaacs, and Samantha

Messier (assistant managers), Ed Shaw (night manager), Damian DeAngelis (restaurant manager), Chef Ben Schneller, assistant restaurant managers Juli Manring and Dan Smith, bar manager Kassi Dolson and her predecessor Richie Bagdasarian. I would also like to thank all of our loyal frontline people, reservationists, restaurant housekeeping and maintenance staff, including longtime standouts like Dexter, Bob, Wally, Michael B., Michael T., Jimmy, Scott, Maria, Naomi, Boomer, Heather, James, Megan, Rhonda, Tim, Johnny B., John L., Kathy, Samantha B., Manny, Amber, Marianne, Heather B., Jenna Rose, Greg and Bob at the pool, Juan and so many others that we have failed to mention. Everyone was important.

We would like to thank our architects, Peter Pike and Michael Ingram; our contractors Mingo Castellanos, Tim Roof, Gary Loer and Marshall White, and the elected and appointed government personnel in Key West who gave us so much support.

We want to express our gratitude also to our bankers Marianne VanWulfen, Farris Kalil, and their colleagues at Michigan National Bank and its many successors, and Dale Bittner at BB&T who gave us their financial support. We also thank Larry Wolfe and Adam Etra of Eastdil Realty who, along with our attorney Scott Fuerst, represented us so admirably in the sale.

Dale extends his gratitude to his wife Robyn for her loyalty and support to the hotel and to him throughout his time with the Southernmost Hotel Collection and well beyond.

Stuart also wants to send a thank you to his wife Susan for taking on the role of Hotel Ambassador and spending countless hours at the pools, going out of her way to meet and talk with as many guests as possible, making them feel important, special and welcomed. Her efforts to discover, and make sure our staff properly acknowledged, any special occasions that a guest might be celebrating was so helpful in maintaining our culture of care.

Our special thanks goes to our talented Elisa, who was instrumental in making the Southernmost Hotel Collection great and took on the challenge of writing this case study.

And of course we extend our gratitude to our loyal, as well as occasional, clientele. Without your patronage, amazing support and wonderful comments to the world, we would have nothing to write about. Thank you everyone.

ABOUT THE AUTHORS

ELISA LEVY

ELISA LEVY HAS BEEN TEACHING SEMINARS throughout the U.S. and abroad for almost two decades. Her clients run the gamut from United Nations staff in Africa, the Middle East and Europe, to fortune 500 executives and non profit organizations in the United States. She is the author of two books, journal articles and training manuals. She lives in Key West with her husband and daughter.

STUART KAUFMAN AND DALE RANDS

STUART KAUFMAN AND DALE RANDS were the co-managing directors of the company that owned and operated the

Southernmost Hotel Collection in Key West, Florida. In 1970, Stuart and Dale became partners in a law firm in downtown Detroit Michigan. They left the law firm in mid 1980s to pursue their entrepreneurial spirit. In addition to the hotel business their business activities included real estate acquisition and development, ownership and operation of a broadcasting company, a mill working company, and numerous other ventures. Dale resides in West Palm Beach with his wife, Robyn. Stuart and his wife, Susan, live in Key West, Florida.

Stuart Kaufman (left center) and Dale Rands (right center) with Southernmost Hotel Collection Staff

Made in the USA
Columbia, SC
12 March 2020

89078157R00126